# Writing for Your Peers

# Writing for Your Peers

## The Primary Journal Paper

Sylvester P. Carter

New York
Westport, Connecticut
London

**Library of Congress Cataloging-in-Publication Data**

Carter, Sylvester P.
  Writing for your peers.

  Includes index.
  1. Technical writing.   I. Title.
T11.C329        1987        808 '.0666        87-2513
ISBN 0-275-92630-3  (alk. paper)
ISBN 0-275-92229-4  (pbk. : alk. paper)

Library of Congress Catalog Card Number: 87-2513
ISBN: 0-275-92630-3
ISBN: 0-275-92229-4   (pbk)

First published in 1987

Praeger Publishers, 521 Fifth Avenue, New York, NY 10175
A division of Greenwood Press, Inc.

Printed in the United States of America

∞

The paper used in this book complies with the
Permanent Paper Standard issued by the National Information
Standards Organization (Z39.48-1984).

10  9  8  7  6  5  4  3  2  1

*To my dear wife Agnes, without whose
encouragement and patience this book
would never have been completed.*

# Contents

*Foreword*     *ix*

*Preface*     *xi*

*Acknowledgments*     *xiii*

**1**    *The Journal Paper*     *1*

**2**    *The Introduction*     *23*

**3**    *Theoretical Material*     *45*

**4**    *Experimental Material*     *65*

**5**    *Openings and Closings*     *83*

**6**    *Taking and Giving Credit*     *100*

*Appendix A*     *117*

*Appendix B*     *119*

*Appendix C*     *121*

*Notes*     *123*

*Index*     *125*

# *Foreword*

When you invent, struggle with sorting out raw ideas, you talk to yourself. For many people, including myself, this lonely period is nonverbal: mental images are floating around in your head, and at some point, if you are lucky enough, the pieces come together.

Take another situation and observe a team while developing something which has never been. Their conversations sound incomprehensible to you, yet they understand each other through signs, strange images on the blackboard, the jargon they created during their many creative sessions. It takes a long while until all this stops, and every team member agrees that the job is complete.

Unfortunately the job is far from being complete. Sy Carter's book is about the even harder work which follows scientific discovery or engineering innovation, a period which needs another kind of creativity, the one necessary to tell outsiders about results. And this is the period in which most scientists and engineers are rather helpless: the symbols, the jargon, the vague signs so useful during the technical work become meaningless, and may even draw criticism for being incomprehensible, indeed confusing.

There is obviously no need to explain here why communicating scientific and technical progress must go beyond the small group involved with its creation. What is not so well understood is, however, that this communication must help efficient *reading and comprehending* by colleagues who are outside the creator's subculture.

Carter's approach to increasing efficiency consists of two parts: first, the overall efficiency, the agreement on the structure, an almost-standard way of organizing material. Clearly, if all journal papers have the same structure, the reader has a much easier time to find a piece of information, or to jump from one part to another, in the process of *understanding* the entire material. The second is the efficiency with which the different sections of the paper can be understood by the reader, down to the level of symbols used and notations applied.

I wish I had had this book on my desk over the decades while struggling with the articulation of new ideas which appeared so clear to me and, after having put them down, sounded so confusingly presented and fuzzy to others. At that time, I had a friend instead, the editor of a journal, the gentle guide, who patiently helped put the material in clear text, which finally allowed my ideas to penetrate other peoples' minds. I recommend that you keep my friend's book, *Writing for Your Peers,* on your desk.

L. A. Belady
Vice President and Program Director
Microelectronics and Computer Technology Corp.
Austin, Texas

# *Preface*

"It's a cultural thing." This remark was made by a referee from a leading university. It was his explanation for two significant problems that persisted in the second version of a journal submission. Despite objections raised about the original manuscript, the author continued to sprinkle his paper with promotional words and phrases. Moreover, he demonstrated a disturbing inability to distinguish between the trivial and the significant.

Some prospective journal authors would like to be given a formula for avoiding all such problems. Indeed, many books and articles about writing seem to promise such a panacea. The reality is, however, that there is no equation for writing good journal papers. Many of the individual decisions that must be made are based on an acquired "feel" for what is expected. That feel is usually assimilated over a long period of time, and the experienced author may not even be conscious of its origins. It is shaped by the training the author received as a scientist or engineer, by he or she having read many journal papers, and even by the sometimes harsh criticisms of referees and editors about past writing efforts.

This book is intended to shorten the learning time for new authors, to make it less painful, and also to enhance the productivity and the quality of the output of more experienced authors. The book is based on a few assumptions. Because journal papers report original results, their authors are likely to be both creative and intelligent. If this book is successful in communicating the principles on which the practices followed in journal papers are based, prospective authors should be able to apply those principles to make the many decisions required in writing every journal paper. Although we do provide specific recommendations and examples, we also recognize that we cannot address every situation that might arise.

Accordingly, Chapter 1 attempts to explain the purpose of the journal paper in the world of science and technology and to identify those characteristics that so clearly distinguish it from other writing forms. We hope that this immersion into the cultural milieu of journal publication will help our author-readers to make realistic judgments about their own papers as well as those of others. In this instance, we intend "realistic" to mean consistent with the reactions of most other readers of the same paper, including its referees.

The theme established in Chapter 1, that writing journal papers is easier if authors thoroughly understand their function, is carried through for the remainder of the book. Each element of the paper is considered in terms of its purpose. The kinds of information needed to fulfill that purpose are then discussed.

This approach to writing journal papers provides the flexibility needed to document contributions to a wide range of disciplines. By allowing our readers to share in the reasoning process (just as readers of journal papers should be able to do), they are given the opportunity to agree or to disagree with our recommendations. If a reader understands our reasons for suggesting that a certain kind of information be provided at a certain place in the paper, he or she may conclude that the documentation of a particular contribution would be better served by providing it somewhere else or by not providing it at all.

And we do hope that readers of this book will think seriously enough about our recommendations to question them. We do not have all the answers in this intriguing but complex area, and those readers who do take issue with what we say may be in an excellent position to advance further the art of writing journal papers. The staggering progress in science and technology, and the corresponding massive increases in technical literature, demand greater efficiency in both the documentation process itself and in the effectiveness of communicating the results of research through the medium of the journal paper.

# Acknowledgments

Two former associates significantly influenced my attitudes about writing in general and about writing journal papers in particular. The first was the late Jack Wolfram, formerly of Univac, IBM, and Honeywell. Jack was himself a superb writer and was also the ultimate realist about writing. He made me realize how insignificant many of the issues really are that occupy the time and thoughts of many writers and editors. The bottom line for Jack was always how well writing satisfied its basic purpose. The other is Lyle Johnson of IBM. Lyle was editor of the *IBM Systems Journal* at a time when the mission of that publication was the documentation of original results in computer science. Although I had had considerable experience as a writer and editor before I joined the staff of the *Systems Journal,* it was Lyle who introduced me to the conventions followed in primary journal papers. This sometimes painful initiation made me realize how little most seasoned writers and editors really know about journal publication.

My convictions about journal publication were also shaped by the countless anonymous referees whose reports I studied over the years, with the views of these unsung heroes and heroines of the journal publication process seeping into my consciousness. Indeed, it was the remarkable consistency in the reactions of these independent reviewers that first motivated me to try to identify those writing characteristics that were highly valued in journal papers.

I am grateful also to my management at the IBM Corporation for their support and encouragement and for access to the amazing text processing facilities that were used in preparing the manuscript.

Finally, I am deeply indebted to the following people for giving so generously of their time and talent to comment on the many drafts of the various chapters of the book: Irving Ames, Les Belady, Susan Carter, Al Davis, Harlow Freitag, Lyle Johnson, Erik Klokholm, John Lacy, Gerald Mahoney, Richard Parmelee, Phylis Reisner, Marty Schatzoff, and Connie Seddon. However, responsibility for the opinions expressed rests entirely with the author.

# 1

# *The Journal Paper*

An essential requirement of scientific and technological progress is that physicists, computer scientists, engineers, physiologists, and behavioral scientists, among others, document their original findings for the benefit of their peers. The vehicle typically used for this purpose is the journal paper. The publications in which such papers appear may simply be called journals, but the word journal is sometimes modified by adjectives such as primary, archival, scholarly, learned, or refereed. These names distinguish such periodicals from those that use the word journal in their titles but are not restricted to reporting original results. In this book, we sometimes borrow the term *primary journal*.

We hope that the following discussion of the purpose and characteristics of the primary journal paper will help aspiring authors to make decisions that will result in more efficient and effective communication of their results. We hope also that some of the principles discussed will be used in other factual literature, because it is our conviction that communication in general would be enhanced by their application.

There is surprising agreement among journal readers, regardless of discipline, about what constitutes good writing in a journal paper. If two regular readers of a journal were to conclude independently that a particular paper was well written, it is our experience that most other readers of that paper would concur with their judgment. We think that this nearly unanimous reaction results because journal readers expect to find certain characteristics in the papers they read and that their appraisals depend on the extent to which these properties are present. An obvious first step toward writing good journal papers then is identification of these characteristics.

Journal papers are clearly different from, for example, repair manuals. But they are also different from the often beautifully written articles that appear in publications like *Scientific American*. Journal papers are not just more esoteric, more mathematical, and possibly more difficult to read. Journal papers are written differently because they play a fundamentally different role in the world of science and technology, and it is this role that gives rise to their distinctive characteristics.

In the first of three sections in this chapter, we attempt to acquaint readers with the primary journal paper and to identify its niche in the research and development environment. Topics discussed include the measures taken to ensure the correctness of the information documented, other ways of reporting new findings, the kinds of results that might be reported, some criteria typically applied in judging submissions, and the implications of good writing on the acceptability of journal papers. In the next section, three special concerns of the author of a journal paper are considered: scientific rigor, professional ethics, and efficient communication. In the final section, we discuss some topics that might make the task of writing journal papers easier: the process of writing, the possibility of further standardization of the journal paper, and the parts of a typical journal paper and the purposes they serve. The elements of the journal paper are examined in considerably greater detail in succeeding chapters.

We look at journal papers somewhat idealistically, especially in this chapter. Even the best actual journal papers only approximate the ideal. However, some grasp of principles is essential to provide direction to the inexperienced author, who is often confused by the variety of objections to early attempts at journal paper authorship. Nonetheless, after authors have gained experience (and the confidence that usually accompanies it), knowing departures from generally accepted practices can sometimes result in a paper more suited to documenting a particular result.

## THE FORMAL DOCUMENTATION OF NEW RESULTS

The primary journal has evolved as the medium typically used by researchers to record formally for their peers the original results of their investigations.[1] Their discoveries may in fact have been made known before their appearance in a journal paper. For example, they may have been revealed in press releases, in company reports, or at technical conferences. But in submitting a paper to a primary journal, the author is asserting that he or she has extended knowledge in the discipline in a nontrivial way, and the paper must include sufficient evidence to demonstrate to an audience of peers the validity of the claims. Indeed, it ought to be possible for other investigators to follow the reasoning of the author, to duplicate the experiments, and to arrive at the same conclusions as did the author.

**The Testing Process**

Before publication, to confirm that the results described in a journal paper deserve archival recording, the paper is reviewed by the author's peers in the "refereeing process." Typically, two or three active contributors to the author's discipline are asked by the editor to comment on the originality and significance (and implicitly on the correctness) of the results reported, usually with the understanding that their identities will not be revealed to the author. The reactions of the referees are generally provided anonymously to the author by the editor, who, based largely on their guidance, may decide to publish the paper as is, to request its revision, or to reject it.

Appearance of a paper in a primary journal constitutes "formal" publication, and it implies that the scientific evidence in the paper was adequate to convince its referees of the soundness of the findings. However, the testing does not end with publication. The very form and content of the journal paper are intended to expose the author's results, and, equally important, how they were arrived at, to all active workers in the discipline. Because further work may be based on the discoveries reported, some of these readers will carefully examine the theoretical arguments of the author and consider the inferences made from the experimental data to assure themselves of the correctness of the results. Indeed, a few of these readers may attempt to duplicate them. Thus, journal publication can be seen as an integral part of the total process of scientific and technological development, with claimed advances to knowledge made available to the author's peers for their inspection and use, and also with the hope that publication of each good result will stimulate further research.

*Value of Refereeing to the Author*

Inexperienced authors might think that all the testing associated with journal publication would be an ordeal for authors. Although this is sometimes the case, researchers usually welcome useful reactions from referees. Peer review is an integral part of doing the work as well as documenting the results. Science and technology have grown increasingly complex as our understanding of the world around us has expanded and deepened. Extensions to present knowledge and solutions to as-yet-unsolved problems are seldom simple. Thus, authors need the assistance of their professional colleagues to assure them that there are no serious errors in their results or in the foundations on which they are based. And beyond protecting the author from the embarrassment of publishing a flawed result, it is not unusual for referees to suggest useful extensions and improvements to the work. Moreover, although referees seldom recommend publication without change, authors are usually grateful also for their assistance in eliminating some of the less significant lapses that seem to mar every journal submission.

## Related Technical Literature

The primary journal paper has several close relatives, and there are variations in the publication criteria applied by different journals. For example, provision is made in some journals for reporting quickly, in the form of "notes" or "communications," potentially important preliminary findings that have not been subjected to the degree of testing normally associated with journal publication. Entire publications are sometimes given over to such articles (see, for instance, *Applied Physics Letters*[2]).

Some journals associated with engineering disciplines accept papers in which the author describes designs and justifies design trade-offs with informal logical arguments. Experimental proof may be limited to a happy coincidence of parameter values in a single piece of equipment. Although this is not the "hard" scientific evidence normally associated with journal papers, if the author makes clear the genre of such a paper in its title and abstract, readers are not likely to be disappointed if the paper provides them with useful information.

Work in progress is often described at technical conferences. Often refereed versions of conference papers or abstracts summarizing oral conference presentations are published later in "conference proceedings," which are usually regarded as part of the formal literature.

The terms "survey" and "review" are used loosely to describe a variety of technical articles, a few of which may be acceptable in publications characterized as primary journals. For example, in an emerging area of investigation, the need for unifying information may be satisfied by a suitable survey paper. One requirement for acceptance by a primary journal is that the insights and relationships revealed must be useful to the author's active peers, rather than simply to those who have failed to stay abreast of the literature. Also, development of the material in the paper must have required original thinking of the author, not just hard work at the library.

Surveys, reviews, and "overviews" that do not satisfy these criteria often form a part of the general technical literature. In environments where publication is closely related to career advancement, it is sometimes said that such articles provide a means for publication to those who do not have an original result to report. Nonetheless, well written articles of this kind can be useful in bringing generally qualified but inactive readers in a specialized area "up to speed." However, they are not intended for an audience doing the leading edge work in the area and thus cannot be classified as primary journal papers.

Obviously, a survey of work done at a particular university or within a given corporation, for example, even if it is directed to an audience of active peers, is seldom of sufficient breadth to justify inclusion in a primary journal. Indeed, such articles may give an unbalanced and misleading picture of the area they are intended to cover.

We call another document that may be written for the author's peers a "technical essay." In such articles, authors who are active in their specialties typically express informed but unsupported opinions. Such articles sometimes play an important function in research and development by advancing ideas that can stimulate further research. However, the absence of scientific corroboration disqualifies them as primary journal papers.

It should be noted also that the word "originality" used in connection with journal papers applies to the technical results, not simply to a fresh approach taken to describe them. The latter, especially when combined with exceptional breadth of knowledge in an area of specialization, may be highly desirable in authors of "tutorials." But in the absence of an original contribution, such articles cannot be regarded as primary journal papers.

## Scope of Our Treatment

Many other kinds of technical documents exist that serve a wide range of purposes.[3,4] Occasionally they are even published in the same periodical with papers that report original results. Here, however, we do not treat explicitly articles that do not possess in reasonable measure the qualities that we associate with primary journals, although much of what is said may be applicable in their preparation. And we do not consider at all scholarly works in fields unrelated to application of the scientific method, such as history and literature.

## Reportable Results

The primary journal paper has long been associated with documenting and reporting new results from scientific research. In addition, many disciplines have associated with them a body of relatively permanent information, additions to which are documented in archival journals. In engineering activities, the kind of information that we have in mind is sometimes called "transferable technology." It is typified by the material ultimately provided in engineering handbooks. Indeed, the kinds of results that are reported in journal papers are often of sufficiently general and enduring interest to later appear in book form.

For example, a fundamentally better general procedure for designing electric motors might provide the basis for a journal paper. Conversely, an article describing how a particular electric motor was designed, even one with characteristics different from any other motor in existence, might not be. The design of the motor might represent a routine application of existing knowledge, an activity that is expected of engineers in their everyday work. Similarly, a different implementation of a known concept (even one for which a patent has been issued) is not necessarily fundamental enough to provide the basis for a journal paper. In general, the suitability for publication in primary journals of papers that report the application of known principles is heavily dependent on the amount of innovation involved. The difficulty of the work and the usefulness of the information may be given some, but usually considerably less, weight.

We agree that contributions to engineering and to the social sciences, ones that teach important lessons to their authors' active peers, are directly comparable to extensions to knowledge in the physical sciences and should be documented in journal papers. But we also think that closer adherence in such documents to some of the practices typically followed in scientific papers might ease some of our severe communication problems by more efficient reporting of more carefully arrived at results.[3,4]

## Judging Contributions

In this book, we generally assume that the author has a good result to report, but, for the sake of completeness, we now consider some of the factors typically involved in evaluating journal submissions. Even if the evidence supporting the claims made in a paper is assumed to be sound, judging contributions is a difficult part of the formal documentation process. People familiar with the requirements for journal publication can sometimes recognize that a particular paper is unsuitable. For example, the article might be a tutorial or the author might simply have described how a product was designed, with no claims made for an original result. However, the opposite judgment, that a paper is acceptable, is much more difficult to make. It requires, at the outset, deep and current knowledge of the field, as well as of the expectations of journal readers. It also requires that the reviewer be sufficiently imaginative to recognize the worth of an unconventional contribution and sufficiently skeptical to recognize a subtly defective one.

### Some Criteria

As indicated earlier, referees are asked to comment on the significance as well as the originality of the claimed contribution. The difficulty of assessing significance is evidenced by the many cases in which the importance of a discovery was not recognized until long after it was made. Actually, how well a result withstands the test of time is a good measure of its importance, but journal editors expect referees to respond before this test can be completed.

Opinions about significance, which are always somewhat subjective, usually involve a combination of criteria. For example, although the claims made in the paper appear to be sound, the result may nonetheless be such a trivial and obvious extension to present knowledge that the expenditure of precious journal space to document it is not justified. Or referees and editors might conclude that a new result is sufficiently important to warrant publication of, say, a six-page paper, but not a ten-page one. And even if a contribution is obvious, if it is also difficult to achieve (a brute force solution), it becomes more acceptable with the degree of difficulty and the value of the information. But an "elegant" result is more desirable.

Some extensions to present knowledge may be well received by scientists because, for example, they explain many previous observations. Other results may arouse little scientific interest but may have immense commercial or social importance. Thus, the editorial objectives of the journal for which the paper is intended also influence judgments about its suitability for publication.

A result that is not obvious, one requiring considerable creativity or ingenuity of the author, is a requirement for publication in many highly esteemed journals. A "seminal" paper, one that reveals many avenues for further research, one likely to be referred to often and for a long period of time in subsequent papers, is looked upon with the greatest favor by referees and editors.

## Prestigious Journals

In addition to variations in the editorial missions of journals, quality requirements also vary widely, with a clear relationship between high standards for acceptance and prestige. It is in the author's interest that the paper be published in the most prestigious journal that will accept it. Among possible benefits are greater likelihood that the results will be seen by the leading members of the discipline and better refereeing.

## Quality of Writing

Journal papers must be written well enough to allow an assessment of the contribution and an evaluation of the supporting scientific foundation. In our experience, the formal documentation of many good results has been delayed or even prevented because their presentation failed to meet such minimum requirements. However, journal papers are working documents. There is no doubt that beautiful writing enhances the likelihood of acceptance. However, the significance of the results and the adequacy of their scientific underpinnings are infinitely more important. Indeed, if the contribution is sufficiently attractive, many minor shortcomings in the writing are easily overlooked. Less significant results do become more acceptable as the length of the paper reporting them decreases, but there is no way that polished writing can compensate for an unoriginal, trivial, or flawed result.

However, there is a relationship between clear, concise writing and the situation of the unknown author that ought not to be overlooked. New findings presented orally at technical conferences, or even informally in conversation, by the leaders in a discipline may be accepted by their peers with little question. The results of less well established workers documented in journal papers are apt to be scrutinized with far more care. The more obstacles to learning about the new findings created by poor writing, the less likely it is that the unknown author's good results will be recognized.

## THREE CHARACTERISTICS OF THE JOURNAL PAPER

Because of the difficulties new authors have in assimilating the conventions followed in journal papers, we now examine some general characteristics associated with these documents. Beyond the fact that the subject matter always involves original knowledge, the most important difference between a journal paper and other technical literature may already have become apparent. The journal author may not include unsupported claims of new discoveries; he or she is obliged to supply enough corroboration so that readers can form their own conclusions about the correctness of the results. We elaborate shortly on the need of the journal author to be continually conscious of *scientific rigor*.

Another distinguishing characteristic of the journal paper is the author's need to be concerned with *professional ethics*. Although some common departures from the rules do not seriously damage the author's professional reputation, persistent violations can be harmful.

The remaining characteristic, *efficiency* in the reporting of new findings, stems from the peculiar requirements of journal readers. Few other forms of writing place as much emphasis on efficient, accurate communication as does the primary journal paper. It caters in a variety of ways directly to its readers' need to learn quickly—but no more painfully than necessary—of the many new discoveries in their field.

### Scientific Rigor

Epistemology has been defined as "that branch of philosophy which is concerned with problems of the nature, limits, and validity of knowledge."[5] Thinking people have been interested, not just in knowing, but in knowing how we know, for thousands of years. At this time in the history of human development, the "scientific method" is the generally accepted means for arriving at the truth, at least where publication of journal papers is concerned.

Exactly what constitutes the scientific method may not be quite as clear-cut as we imagined when first exposed to it in general science classes. There are countless ways in which investigators can delude themselves into believing that they have discovered something new when they have not. However, probably beginning with Galileo,[6] the need for controlled experiments carried out with scrupulous care to verify the predictions of hypotheses has become widely accepted.

## Limits of the Scientific Method

Ideally, new results documented in journal papers should have been arrived at in complete conformance with accepted scientific standards. But, in practice, the scientific method cannot always be applied in the straightforward way described in textbooks. For example, medical investigators, engineers, sociologists, and astronomers are often not free to conduct the kinds of controlled experiments ideally suited to confirming their hypotheses. Data may have to be gathered using less direct means, including computer simulation, probabilistic modeling, and an endless variety of innovative experimental arrangements. Information acquired by such means may be documented and applied simply because it is the best that is available. And workers must be able to communicate such results to fellow investigators, both to motivate further research and to be applied in practice. Under these circumstances, however, authors of journal papers must describe their assumptions and approximations clearly enough so that readers can determine just how much confidence to put in their results.

## Unscientific Evidence

A different kind of departure from complete rigor is much less acceptable in journal submissions but all too common in practice. Despite the ascendency of the scientific method during the past few centuries, we are all exposed to great quantities of less carefully arrived at information. Newspapers, advertisements, trade magazines, our associates at work, our friends, and our families are all supplying us with information and attempting as well to persuade us of its correctness. The tactics used to convince us are so varied and sometimes so subtle that we are often persuaded, not only of the correctness of the information, but of the means of persuasion as well. Thus, we ourselves adopt similar means to influence the thinking of others. If these means have been successful in other areas of our lives, we may inadvertently use them in journal papers. For example, if some unscientific arguments used in a sales pitch to get corporate or government funding for a research project were successful, an investigator might use the same arguments in a journal paper.

Physical and social scientists, engineers, and mathematicians attempt to put aside unscientific evidence, in their papers as well as in their work, not only because it might fail to convince readers of the correctness of their results, but also to avoid deceiving themselves. Indeed, one reason that good researchers want competent refereeing is to assure themselves that they have succeeded. Authors of journal papers are expected to advance sound arguments in support of their conclusions. But if an author unwittingly uses too many unscientific "selling" devices, confidence in the paper can be damaged. Promotional arguments in journal papers instantly lower credibility. Appeals to emotion or prejudice, for example, even if the results are correct, can cause readers to be concerned about undetected flaws in the ways the author has "gotten at the truth." In practice, journal readers must accept some things on faith, for in reality the ideal of duplicating the author's work and arriving at the same conclusions that he did is often not practical. If anything about a paper arouses suspicion, it is far easier for readers to simply dismiss it. Moreover, since the paper, especially in the case of an unknown author, is the primary evidence of that author's work available to readers, they may even form more general opinions about the author's competence. Future papers by the same author may be ignored by busy journal readers.

### The Author's Obligation

Authors cannot depend on the scrutiny of referees and editors to remove offending material. Although many referees and editors are conscientious, not all of them are. Moreover, the time that they can spend on an individual paper is often limited. Indeed, the availability of papers that present fewer hazards may dissuade them from even bothering. But the worst possibility for the beginning author is that faulty results might be published. Thus, aspiring authors must develop their own critical faculties.

### An Example

Because so far this discussion has been somewhat abstract, we now look at a simple example from an actual journal paper. The submission was from several engineers, with good academic credentials, who had previously made some important contributions. Both the abstract of the paper and its introduction informed readers that a testing procedure to be reported had been accepted as a standard throughout the large corporation that employed them. But standardization often has inherent benefits independent of the merits of the chosen procedure. For example, training costs might be lower if the most widely used method were adopted universally, even if it were not the best. In a business organization, the choice might actually have had political motivation. In this case, indicating the widespread adoption of their method, done presumably to win the favor of readers, could well have the opposite of the intended effect, especially if combined with other promotional arguments.

**Professional Ethics**

The primary product of many researchers is the journal paper and the original ideas it represents. Recognition, career advancement, tenure, even employment may depend on the number of papers published and sometimes also on which journals accepted them.[3] It is not surprising then that there is often intense competition for journal space and the recognition for scientific achievement that publication implies. Original results are often not patentable, for example, in the social and computer sciences. Without a generally accepted code of ethics to protect discoveries, an epidemic of conflicts among researchers would undoubtedly occur. Investigators would become more reluctant to reveal new results, and scientific and technological progress would be seriously hampered.

*Varieties of Lapses*

Most of us are aware of career-destroying scandals of the type periodically reported in newspapers and magazines.[7] These cases usually involve deliberate falsification of experimental results, and referees and editors must certainly be alert to this possibility. However, we do not concern ourselves here with what we hope is the small percentage of researchers who engage in fraud. We have no recommendations either for investigators who are so eager for recognition that they delude themselves, and we can only hope that the refereeing system will prevent formal documentation of their questionable results.

Another category of improprieties results from the inexperience of authors, who unwittingly violate the rules. For example, beginning authors may submit the same paper to more than one journal without informing the editors; or they may neglect to attribute an idea expressed in their paper to its originator, thereby implying that it is their own.

Mildly unethical behavior often results when authors try too hard to promote their careers through their papers. For example, such authors might refer to their own earlier papers even though they have no bearing on the present result or might include as a coauthor a high-ranking person in their organization who contributed nothing to the work. Several different papers might be published reporting slightly disguised versions of the same result. We recall an instance in which an author implied in his acknowledgments that a respected colleague viewed his work with favor; the colleague told us, however, that he discussed only one aspect of the work with the author and had never seen the complete paper. In any case, the favorable opinion of an authority is not scientific evidence.

It is probably evident that unethical and unscientific practices can sometimes be difficult to distinguish. The question may be one of whether the author is fooling himself or herself or attempting to fool others. Moreover, practices that may be acceptable in other areas of the author's life may not be in journal papers. For example, some of the truth may be suppressed in proposals designed to win contracts and in other sales literature, in ways that would not be acceptable in a journal paper.

It may also be interesting to note that self promotion in the journal publication process is not limited to authors. Some referees can be counted on to recommend in their reports that the author refer to some of the referee's previous papers, no matter how tenuously they are related to the paper under review.

*The Consequences of Lapses*

Offenses resulting from ignorance or excessive zeal are not usually catastrophic. Readers may simply conclude that the author is naive or has displayed bad judgment. Not giving credit to another investigator for an idea is a serious breach of professional ethics, but even here, if the offense was inadvertent, the author is not likely to suffer long-term consequences. A pattern of such improprieties, however, can be professionally damaging. Such misdemeanors are often obvious to sophisticated journal readers, and fellow investigators do discuss the tendencies of their colleagues to commit them. An author who engages in these practices may even find few opportunities in the future for collaboration with wary colleagues.

## Efficient Reporting of New Findings

Journal audiences are not likely to be composed of casual readers, because the papers they read often have direct influence on their own investigations. But researchers are obliged to do a great deal of reading to remain informed of new discoveries in their fields. The much-talked-about information explosion could completely overwhelm them and seriously impede scientific and technological progress without a reasonably efficient means for documenting and communicating new results. Many properties of primary journal papers help to avoid such a catastrophe.

The concept of the journal itself reduces significantly the amount of reading required of researchers. The reader of a "respectable" journal is provided reasonable assurance of getting new information, since the author by convention is usually constrained from sending the same paper to more than one journal (see *Scholarly Communication* for a discussion of proposed exceptions[3]). Moreover, the refereeing process is intended to ensure the correctness and significance, as well as the originality, of the reported findings. Thus, the refereeing process, combined with the scientific support for new knowledge expected of a journal paper, provide greater assurance that reading effort will be rewarded with sound, significant, original results.

*Superfluous Information*

One measure of the "goodness" of a journal paper is the amount of new material provided per page. The terse expression characteristic of journal paper style has gotten considerable attention in books and articles about writing.[8,9] Examples are often provided of cleverly rewritten sentences that convey the same information as did their cumbersome and wordy original counterparts. We are in sympathy with this approach generally, although a few authors carry it to such extremes that the reading effort avoided is more than offset by the intellectual effort added. However, too little attention has been given to a related and more common problem.

Information may be expressed lucidly and tersely, but may at the same time be completely extraneous in terms of the purpose of a journal paper. Regardless of the justifications offered by authors for retaining it, this irrelevant information adds to reading effort without a commensurate return in the kinds of information that journal audiences expect, and many journal readers are impatient with papers that contain it. Common examples are background material not needed by the audience for the particular paper and textbook information to which all of the author's peers were at one time exposed. Repeating such information in every paper in a particular specialty seriously degrades efficiency. Extracting unessential information from a paper after it has been written may be painful for the author, but the consequences of retaining it may be even worse.

*Possible Consequences*

Our conviction about the desirability of excluding extraneous information is based on an observation. We have seen numerous instances in which referee reaction to the results reported in the original version of a paper was lukewarm at best. A revised version of the same paper, with no information essential to a journal paper added or deleted, but with considerable irrelevant information removed, was enthusiastically received by the same referees. Apparently, the impact of a good result can be so diluted by superfluous information that its most careful readers underestimate its worth. Moreover, many readers of papers containing irrelevant information probably overlook some of the valuable new ideas they contain.

(Verbose authors are sometimes penalized by the practice of many professional societies of imposing a page charge to help defray the costs of publication. However, this motivation for brevity is nullified if the organization with which the author is affiliated pays the page charge.)

*Further Reductions in Reading Effort*

Experienced journal authors take care in the writing of titles, abstracts, and introductions to describe precisely the nature and bounds of their contributions. If journal papers do not promise more than they deliver, readers are more likely to be rewarded for their effort than are readers of much other literature.

The journal paper is directed at the author's active peers, who are assumed to be familiar with the current literature in their field. As mentioned before, the time wasted in the needless rereading of familiar material is thus reduced. Also, it is only necessary to go down to a level of detail beyond which these readers can carry on for themselves.

The way that journal papers are organized has become somewhat stylized, which can be helpful in matching reading effort to reader requirements. For example, those readers who wish only to know what the author has discovered, but are not interested in examining the proofs, may choose not to read beyond the introduction in a well-structured journal paper. A predictable organization also facilitates use of the paper for reference purposes.

## The Need for Lucid Writing

Reading effort can sometimes be reduced even further by a means so prosaic that it might be overlooked. The subject matter of many journal papers is inherently difficult, and serious readers expect to expend intellectual effort to understand it. However, a paper ought to be written so that it is no more difficult to understand than the subject matter requires. For example, if more careful writing can reduce the reading time of 2,000 readers an average of 15 minutes, the 500 hours saved by the scientific community would seem to justify many hours of additional effort on the part of the author to present and justify the results more clearly. In our experience, most successful authors do strive for clarity and precision, as well as economy, in reporting their new findings, even though it is the findings themselves that have made these authors successful.

## Some Limits on Brevity

It should be noted also that efficient communication is not achieved by the omission of information needed for comprehension, such as introductory material at the beginnings of subdivisions of the paper. Moreover, planned redundancy may even be necessary, because human beings, unlike computers, do not remember facts indefinitely. Also, the judicious repetition of some kinds of information (for example, in the title, the abstract, and the introduction) may improve efficiency. It not only facilitates understanding, through the journalistic technique of providing greater elaboration in successive presentations of the same information, it also reduces wasted time by screening out readers not likely to profit from further reading. (These notions are explored more deeply in later chapters.)

## WRITING THE JOURNAL PAPER

The writing of the journal paper is part of the total process of scientific and technological development; and the activity of writing, as well as that of reading, ought to be as efficient as possible. By examining introspectively the process of writing, prospective authors may be better able to arrive at the desired goal of a "good" paper while expending less effort than might otherwise be required. In addition, further standardization of the structure and contents of the journal paper might also reduce the work load of authors. Finally, the more clearly authors understand the objectives they are striving to achieve in each of the parts of the paper, the less effort they are likely to waste in writing them.

In the next three subsections, we look more closely at the writing process itself, which involves four separate activities—considering purpose, identifying topics, organizing, and writing. In the second subsection, we consider the possibility of greater standardization of journal papers, regardless of discipline. Benefits for both authors and readers are possible, although excessive rigidity is a hazard. In the final subsection, we discuss the purposes served by each of the parts of a typical journal paper.

### The Process of Writing

An author must, of course, have a clear purpose in mind to write effectively. After consciously establishing a goal for the document, the author can then determine the kinds of information that are needed to achieve it. Equally important, information not relevant for the purpose can be rejected. When the information that must be provided has been identified, a plan for conveying it can be devised—the outline of the document, with appropriate ordering and subordination of topics. (Note that preparing the outline is just one of the activities, other than the writing itself, and not necessarily the first one.) Finally, the author must do the actual writing.

If the resulting document does not achieve its intended purpose (and it rarely does on the first attempt), any or all of these activities are repeated as often as necessary until it does. Even the outline, which some authors regard as sacred once it has been written, may itself have to be altered. Thus, the author moves from one to another of these four activities (considering purpose, identifying topics, organizing, and writing) as the situation requires. In our experience, the order in which they are carried out varies among competent writers. Some authors plunge ahead with a very rough draft early in the process because they feel more comfortable working with existing text. Others prepare detailed outlines before writing a word. If the result is successful, the order in which the four activities are carried out is immaterial. However, it might be useful for those authors who do rush to complete a rough draft to maintain, in parallel with their revising activities, a current written outline. Referring to it occasionally can reduce the likelihood of losing control of the organization.

## *The Work Load of the Author*

Inexperienced authors should not be daunted by the amount of work that seems to be needed to produce an acceptable journal paper. Most published authors would agree that writing the second one is considerably easier than writing the first. Moreover, the author should remember that most journal readers will be far more interested in the significance and validity of the results than in the niceties of English usage in the paper. The fact is that the papers of some well-established investigators contain a rather large number of such trivial lapses.

Writing a journal paper is easier than most other writing in another way as well. Because its purpose remains the same, documenting new results from research, the same kinds of information, and even the same general structure, are suitable for all journal papers. Thus, three of the four activities, establishing purpose, identifying topics, and organizing, have already been at least partly done for the author.

## Standardizing the Journal Paper

Some professional societies suggest in a general way the organization and contents of papers intended for their journals[10-13] (although most attention in these guides seems to be given to stylistic and formatting considerations). Some even make a conscious effort to derive the benefits of standardization while avoiding the stultifying effects of blind conformity.[10] But even in the absence of guidelines for authors, in practice, considerable similarity exists among journal papers in different disciplines.

Further standardization of journal papers could benefit both readers and authors. We have already mentioned a couple of benefits for readers. However, there is an ever present problem of excessively rigid conformance.

In documents governed by specifications, authors are relieved of even more of the activities related to writing. For example, preparing some of the reports required of manufacturers of military equipment approaches filling in the blanks on a form. However, the author may not be free to make choices that could result in more effective communication or even to include material thought to be relevant. Also, writing done under these conditions can be so lacking in spontaneity that retaining reader attention is difficult, probably causing further reductions in information transfer.

Nonetheless, we think that there is enough commonality among papers in all of the physical and social sciences, as well as in mathematics, engineering, and computer science, to allow greater standardization of journal papers. Indeed, the increasing need for communication across discipline boundaries suggests that efficiency in documenting and communicating the results of research would be enhanced by further standardization. The same general kinds of information would be provided in each of the parts of the paper (as we describe them later), even though the contributions might be quite different.

For example, the claims made in an engineering paper might be demonstrated by a combination of logical arguments justifying design choices and experimental data obtained from prototypes or from newly designed equipment, rather than from the designed experiments more typical of scientific papers. And for a result such as a new computer programming language, there might be little question that it can be implemented in a compiler or interpreter capable of converting it into a form that can be understood by a computer. In this case, the author might be obliged instead to convince readers of the expressiveness of the language for particular kinds of applications. Or in a paper providing experimental data believed to have practical value, the major effort might be to demonstrate that the data are actually a valid measure of the phenomenon claimed from them.

Of course, the journal paper must be implemented in particular instances with sufficient flexibility to accommodate the needs of each contribution. For instance, theoretical results should not have to be forced into the format of an experimental paper, as seems to be suggested even in the few useful books about writing journal papers.[14,15] Actually, many good theoretical papers are published every year by respected journals in areas such as mathematics, computer science, and astronomy. Indeed, Einstein's theory of relativity was a theoretical contribution.

Throughout the remainder of this book, we codify and document practices often presently followed in journal papers. But we sometimes depart from existing practice in directions that we think are better, and our detailed recommendations for the kinds of information that should be included in the parts of a journal paper have often originated with us. Unlike the practice followed in journal papers, however, we make no distinction between our ideas and those of others, and we discuss the parts of the paper as though they were now written the way we think they ought to be.

## The Parts of the Journal Paper

Journal papers consist of a number of elements, each of which plays a specific role in providing the unified body of information needed to advise prospective readers of a new result, to describe it, to provide the scientific foundation needed for readers to assure themselves of its correctness, and to give credit to everyone who contributed toward achieving it (including the author). We consider each of these parts here in only enough detail to allow readers to see their purposes and relationships, and for the most part we discuss them in the order in which they might appear in an actual paper. In subsequent chapters, more specific information is provided about each, and they are discussed there in approximately the order that an author might choose to write them.

## The Names of the Authors

Authors' names appearing on a journal paper tell readers who contributed fundamental, innovative ideas to the results reported. Hard but routine work done on large projects, for example, does not justify including a worker's name as an author of a paper stemming from the project. Indeed, routine work would not be described in the paper in the first place.

There is no necessary relationship among the authors' names, the order in which they appear, and who actually did the writing. However, in papers having more than one author, the first-named author may have contributed more importantly to the results reported if the names do not appear alphabetically.

Important concerns of the author are the relative position of his or her name on papers having more than one author and the form in which the name appears, which may be related to establishing the author's professional identity.

## The Title

The title of the paper, and to a slightly lesser extent its abstract, will appear in separately published indexes and information retrieval systems. Thus, the title exposes the author's contribution to more people than does any other part of the paper.

The purpose of the title is to begin focusing the attention of readers onto the specific contribution documented in the paper. Thus, prospective readers can determine whether they are likely to profit from further reading. This purpose is accomplished by providing as many as four kinds of information: the area in which the original contribution is made, the contribution itself and its limits, its significance to the author's discipline, and the general approach used in acquiring the new information or achieving the new result. The first two are always required.

Because of the limited space available in the title, words must be chosen carefully to accomplish its purpose efficiently, and the vocabulary must be appropriate for the expected audience. Authors must also be wary of the possible negative consequences of their word choices. For example, "buzz" words and promotional phrases may deter prospective readers from reading further.

## The Abstract

Author-written abstracts, which, like titles, are often published separately from journal papers themselves, provide additional details beyond those that appeared in the title to help prospective readers to determine their interest in further reading. Thus, one purpose of the abstract is to continue screening readers, the process that was started by the title. Also, because of the immense amount of reading required of researchers in this time of rapid technological progress, many readers rely solely on abstracts to learn about many discoveries in their discipline, reading more only of those papers that are directly related to their own work. It is essential, therefore, that the author provide in the abstract as much information about the contribution as space allows. Moreover, the author should remember that there is a distinction between actually providing information about a contribution in the abstract and merely promising in the abstract to do so in the paper itself.

As was the case with the title, some information may also be included in the abstract to suggest the methodology used and to indicate the significance to the discipline of the new findings.

In a paper reporting an original result, no space should be wasted in the abstract on a verbal outline of the paper.

## The Introduction

The primary purpose of the introduction is to describe fully the author's contribution. Thus, the introduction carries the filtering process of the title and the abstract to its limit. However, the complete description of the contribution in the introduction also entails fitting it into the context of present knowledge about the subject, through the judicious use of references to related current literature.

Introductions may serve subordinate purposes also, such as indicating the significance of the new result—possibly even for readers who are not the author's peers. Because many journal readers do not read beyond the introduction, information intended solely to prepare readers for the body is usually limited to a short preview of the paper included at the end of the introduction.

## The Body

The material that most clearly distinguishes the primary journal paper from other technical literature is included in the body. It is here that the theoretical arguments and the experimental evidence needed to convince the author's peers of the validity of his or her claims are provided.

As many as five kinds of information may be needed for readers to follow the author's reasoning in theoretical passages: the contentions to be proved; underlying assumptions; facts essential to understanding (such as mathematical notation); the theoretical developments themselves; and possibly logical arguments intended to persuade readers that the theory can also be applied in practice despite inadequate empirical evidence.

As many as six kinds of information may be needed in experimental material: statements of the purposes of the experiments; explanations of how their designs accomplish their purposes; descriptions of experimental apparatus and procedures; presentation of experimental data; observations, logical inferences, and informed opinions arising from the data; and discussions of the broader implications of the experimental results for the author's discipline.

Theoretical and experimental information is often combined in the same paper. For example, the author's reasoning about the experimental data may have led to additional experimentation, which in turn led to even deeper theoretical understanding.

It should be noted also that the claims rigorously supported in the bodies of some papers may be quite different from those in the typical physical science paper. For example, in a computer science paper, the author might have to justify contentions of better performance, more efficient use of computer memory, or greater precision of mathematical results. Both theoretical arguments and experimental evidence might be needed to support such claims.

### The Concluding Section

The closing of a journal paper first summarizes what has gone before, reminding readers of how the scientific material provided in the body supports the claims made in earlier parts of the paper. The closing next indicates the implications of the new information to the author's peers, usually more elaborately than was done in previous parts of the paper. Finally, the reader's attention is directed outward to avenues of further exploration. Thus, the closing is almost the corollary of the opening parts, which focused the reader's attention with increasing specificity on the contribution documented in the paper.

### Acknowledgments

Supportive work by others is usually recognized in an acknowledgment section. One decision that an author might have to make is whether an individual should be given credit here or has contributed enough fundamental knowledge to be included as a coauthor. Gratitude for funding may also be expressed in the acknowledgment section, although contractual obligations may require that appreciation be expressed in other ways.

### References

References in journal papers do more than direct readers to further information about a topic. They help the author to describe the contribution by comparing and contrasting it with previously reported findings. References also permit the author to build on information that colleagues have demonstrated to be correct elsewhere in the formal literature.

*Received Dates*

The date that a manuscript was received by a journal, and possibly the date of a major revision, are also included with most published papers; these have implications about the time of origin of the author's discoveries.

*Professional Biographies*

Biographies are usually published with journal papers to establish the academic and professional credentials of the author. Only accomplishments related to the author's professional abilities are provided. Relevant and significant awards and honors may be included, but to avoid the appearance of immodesty, trivial accomplishments should be carefully avoided in the author-written biography.

## SUMMARY

The objective of this chapter was to acquaint readers with the role of the primary journal paper in the world of science and technology, that is, to document new results from research and development and thereby to stimulate further work. We discussed the peer review process for testing the originality and significance of the claimed new results, but we reminded readers that even after publication the journal paper will be examined critically by the author's peers. The kinds of results that might be reported and some criteria used to judge submissions were also discussed. Although beautiful writing was not regarded as a requirement, clear writing was believed to increase the likelihood that the unknown author's good results would be recognized.

Some attention was given to three characteristics of a journal paper that stem directly from the purpose it serves. Although journal papers do report only original and significant advances to knowledge, claims of new information were said not to be enough. The claims had to be carefully supported by scientific corroboration. We regarded this concern with scientific rigor as the single most important distinguishing characteristic of the primary journal paper.

We noted that authors of journal papers had also to be aware of the conventions that have evolved to protect other investigators (and ultimately even the author). Although most minor violations of professional ethics were not regarded as disastrous, it was felt that the cumulative effects of persistent offenses could be damaging.

Another distinguishing characteristic of the journal paper was discussed: its concern with the vast amount of reading required of its audience. Many ways in which needless reading effort is avoided by the journal paper were reviewed, but our readers were also reminded that the provision of introductory information and even judicious repetition can enhance efficiency in communicating the results of research.

The view was expressed that the author's time in preparing the manuscript ought also to be used efficiently. We hoped that this might come about if authors better understood the experience of writing, if the contents and structure of the journal paper were more standardized, and if authors were more fully aware of the roles of the various elements of the journal paper.

*The Remainder of the Book*

Chapter 2 is devoted entirely to the preparation of introductions. Chapter 3 is dedicated to the presentation of theoretical information, one of the two kinds of material that may be provided in the body. The other kind, experimental material, is considered in Chapter 4. Chapter 5 treats openings (titles and abstracts) and closings. Finally, in Chapter 6, the remaining parts of the journal paper are discussed, those parts that are associated with taking and giving credit.

# 2
# *The Introduction*

We think that the introduction is the most important part of the journal paper. Its basic purpose is to describe fully the character and extent of the author's contribution, which should already have been suggested in the title and the abstract. It is largely from this description that referees will assess the originality and significance of the author's results, even though they will eventually want proof of the claims. Moreover, if the paper is published, many readers will not read beyond the introduction (if the title and abstract justify going even that far), and their knowledge of the author's contribution will have been obtained almost solely from this part of the paper.

However, the introduction is also the most difficult part of the paper to write. The general statements typical of introductions are filled with implications. The author must be sure of their universal correctness or appropriately qualify them. It is far easier to describe a step in a chemical process or to explain how a logic circuit functions than it is to make these broad declarations and to make them accurately. Moreover, the general statements typical of introductions often sound trite to the author's peers, because of their familiarity with the subject area. Thus, the inexperienced author is often tempted to plunge into "concrete details." However, providing too much detail too soon can create severe comprehension problems for the reader. In addition, it may mean that the author is becoming prematurely concerned with how the results were obtained, rather than what they are, and is thus failing to achieve the real purpose of the introduction.

In the first of seven sections in this chapter, we define original contributions more completely, discuss the importance of explicitly identifying them in journal papers, give reasons for possible failure to do so, and consider several ways of beginning. In the next section, we discuss the need for relating the new discovery to prior knowledge and the major method used for doing so, that is, by comparing and contrasting it with results previously reported in the current formal literature. Background information is then discussed with the aim of finding a realistic compromise between the needs of the specialist to learn efficiently of new results and the requirements of those not completely conversant with the literature. Whether, for whom, and where authors ought to discuss the significance of their findings is considered in the following section. In the two succeeding sections, we discuss the inclusion in the introduction of hints at the approaches used in getting the new results and of a preview of the structure and contents of the rest of the paper. A few general comments about writing introductions are made in the final section. Appendix A at the end of the book lists criteria that can be used in judging the success of journal paper introductions.

## ACHIEVING THE BASIC PURPOSE OF THE INTRODUCTION

The primary purpose of the introduction to a journal paper is to announce a contribution, with the word *contribution* meaning a significant addition of original information to the store of knowledge in a particular discipline. That new knowledge may be, for example, a basic extension to scientific knowledge, the solution to a long-standing engineering problem, or the provision of data useful to behavioral scientists. Although a journal paper may report multiple contributions, we generally assume in this book that one paper reports one contribution.

We hope that our mention of multiple contributions does not lead readers to equate lists of achievements with contributions. For example, the successful design of a semiconductor memory chip for an original application might have been a major effort that required the achievement of many subgoals. However, the subgoals are only means to an end and by themselves are usually not significant enough to be considered contributions. In the unlikely event that the researcher had discovered and exploited a formerly unknown electrical characteristic of semiconductors in achieving the objective, the paper might then represent two contributions: discovery of the previously unknown property of semiconductors, and an innovative application of semiconductor devices to achieve a previously unattained result.

### Failing to Identify the Contribution

Some of the information needed for the introduction to achieve its purpose of describing the author's discovery was already provided in the title and the abstract. However, too little space was available there to do an adequate job. The title and the abstract, for example, provide limited opportunities to relate the new results to what had been known before. Moreover, the information about the contribution provided earlier was diluted by different kinds of information provided for different purposes. Thus, the introduction presents the author with the first unrestricted opportunity to develop a passage devoted entirely to stating his or her claim of new information.

In practice, however, it is not unusual for journal papers to be rejected, even those from experienced authors, because referees and editors were not able to identify what the author had to contribute. There appear to be at least two general reasons for this situation.

The author may have an unclear understanding of the expectations of journal readers. For example, no effort may have been made in the introduction (or anywhere else in the paper) to distinguish the author's original ideas from other information, making it impossible for readers to identify the original contribution. Or the author might think of the paper as a medium for describing the work but fail to establish what was learned from doing the work. (Authors with this attitude sometimes follow the introduction with a body containing an autobiographical or chronological description of their activities, rather than a demonstration of the validity of any claimed contributions.)

The second general reason for the failure of some authors to provide a distilled description of the basic lesson learned from their research results from mixing motives in the beginning of the introduction. Our remark in the last chapter, that all expository writing can be done more effectively if the author is fully aware of the purpose it is intended to serve, can be extended in an obvious way: The more purposes an author attempts to achieve at the same time, the less well any of them is likely to be achieved. If an author tries to make the beginning of the introduction serve more than its basic purpose of describing the contribution, such as providing a history of the area in which it was made, it is less likely that referees and other readers will be able to identify the contribution itself.

## Some Journal Paper Beginnings

The reader of the introduction is assumed to know nothing of the contribution from having read the title and the abstract. Thus, the beginning of the introduction must focus attention on the specific contribution dealt with in the paper. We discuss here four commonly used strategies for accomplishing this goal: We call them the statement-of-the-contribution beginning, the historical beginning, the statement-of-the-problem beginning, and the statement-of-objectives beginning.

### The Statement-of-the-Contribution Beginning

Some authors begin the introduction with a carefully composed, terse statement that describes exactly the nature and extent of their contributions. (The writing of such a sentence may have added benefits in crystallizing the thinking of the author.) This statement is provided as soon as possible—how soon depending on the particular contribution. For example, if it were claimed that a drug had been discovered that cured all types of cancer, such an assertion could probably be made without preamble. Often, however, the contribution is more specialized, and a few sentences are required to establish a context. For instance, an author might remind readers that the integration of semiconductor devices used in digital computers can result in reduced computer size. A couple of intervening sentences might follow, probably indicating the trend toward denser packaging of circuits. The author might then claim to have found a scheme that allowed heat to be dissipated so well from very large scale integrated circuits that even tighter packaging was now possible, allowing even further reduction in computer size. If the claimed improvements were quantified, readers would be better able to evaluate the contribution.

With this kind of opening, the carefully written statement describing the essence of the contribution provides a framework, and the rest of the first paragraph and probably several succeeding paragraphs or even pages, fill in the details. Thus, in our first example, if a cure had instead been found only for some particular kind of cancer, the author would have to establish exactly which kinds of cancer were affected. Moreover, if the treatment only improved the condition of some patients, the author would have to communicate just how effective it was, so that readers could make judgments about the significance of the contribution. After the author had fully described the result, including its relationship to existing knowledge, he or she might then proceed by discussing the implications of the discovery and by previewing the general structure and contents of the rest of the paper.

The American Mathematical Society advises beginning this way,[10] and we think it is often quite successful in practice. However, it does pose a few problems for the author. One is that the preamble to the statement of the contribution may be composed of trite material well known to expected readers of the paper. (This is probably the case with our circuit packaging example.) In addition, an author may take so long in narrowing the discussion down to his or her own result that readers become impatient; the transition from the known to the unknown must be swift for busy journal readers. There is also some temptation to become involved explicitly with the significance of the new results, when using this or indeed any of the other openings considered here. Discussions of the significance of new results (which we treat later) can introduce confusion into descriptions of the results themselves if not separated from them. Finally, the succinct statement that we have in mind to describe the contribution is often difficult to compose.

*The Historical Beginning*

The historical opening has some similarities to the statement-of-the-contribution beginning. Typically, the paper starts at some turning point in the history of the discipline involved, say, when semiconductors were first used to replace vacuum tubes in computers. After reviews of intervening developments—such as the introduction of transistors and then of integrated circuits, possibly supplemented with quantitative data about corresponding reductions in size and power consumption—this beginning too culminates in a full description of the author's result.

The historical beginning presents the author with the same hazards as the statement-of-the-contribution beginning. But in addition, because historical openings typically provide longer reviews of events well-known to expected readers of a journal paper, there is even greater likelihood of boring busy journal readers.

Nonetheless, historical openings can occasionally be used successfully. For example, they might be appropriate when new results are reported in areas that have long been inactive and for interdisciplinary contributions where the audience may not know the history. However, in a journal paper, the history should be no longer than necessary to provide a smooth and rapid transition to the description of the contribution. It should not be provided for the sake of its possible general interest. Of course, for other kinds of articles and for other audiences, some authors use historical openings very effectively.

## *The Statement-of-the-Problem Beginning*

A third and very popular way to begin the introduction to a journal paper is to describe the problem that was solved. The problem description is intended to provide a context for describing the contribution—its solution. For example, an author might start by asserting that further reductions in the size of computers have not been possible because the heat from more densely packaged circuits would aggravate reliability problems. Several paragraphs of elaboration might follow, with the author providing data to support contentions about the severity of the problem. This opening too should lead naturally to a description of the author's contribution. In our case, the author might finally claim to have devised a very large scale integrated circuit package that allowed more effective dissipation of heat, thus alleviating the problem sufficiently to allow further size reductions. Often, authors using this opening, especially in theoretical papers, would claim to have solved the problem, not just to have improved the situation.

The statement-of-the-problem opening is advocated by the American Chemical Society,[11] by authors of some books about technical writing,[16] and by some instructors of technical writing courses taught to engineers. It has sometimes been recommended as the universal beginning for all journal papers.[15,17]

The statement-of-the-problem opening reflects the attitude of those authors who view their work as solving problems. This may be preferable to thinking of journal papers as media for describing work, since in this case the work is at least directed toward a goal. And with this opening, the new results are almost automatically integrated into the fabric of present knowledge, a requirement we discuss later.

However, solving problems is not the only way of extending knowledge, and in some cases the statement-of-the-problem opening may be completely inappropriate. Journal papers sometimes document findings from research that are not solutions to known problems. Some good results are discovered accidentally. Experimental results published by investigators in the social sciences may pose theoretical questions rather than answer them. Also, experimental data may be provided in journal papers because of their practical value—to engineers, say—even though they do not advance theoretical understanding. Thus, attempting to portray a contribution as the solution to a problem can sometimes sound contrived.

(Some scientists with rather formal attitudes about journal publication might question whether presenting factual information that has not been fitted into a theoretical context is indeed a scientific contribution. However, in this book we recognize the fact that new results that are useful to the author's peers are often documented in journal papers, even though they do not advance theory.)

But even if a problem has been solved, the statement-of-the-problem opening can sometimes weaken the perceived importance of a contribution. One measure of the goodness of a new result is its generality. But here the reader's attention has been focused entirely on the particular problem that was solved, whereas the solution may be far more widely applicable.

Also, authors who use the statement-of-the-problem opening often become so involved with describing the problem (about which their peers may already know) that the reader, after having read the introduction, knows little or nothing about its solution—and it is the solution that is the contribution. Indeed, we have seen submissions in which the author did not even indicate whether the problem was solved until a concluding section at the end of the paper. This practice is sufficiently common so that a former colleague of ours on the staff of the trade magazine *Electronics* often used to convert summaries appearing at the ends of submitted articles into introductions. The statement-of-the-problem opening, then, may delay longer than necessary the reader's learning about the contribution. Postponing the provision of information highly important to readers may be appropriate in mystery stories, but not in journal papers.

Nonetheless, there are a couple of situations in which identification of the problem that was solved can be an effective way to begin. Some unsolved problems are known to virtually all active workers in a particular specialty. Claiming to have solved such classical problems can instantly identify the contribution for the author's peers. But even here, only brief reminders of the problem are needed by the intended audience.

If a more extensive description of the problem seems to be required for some prospective readers (for example, because the paper reports an interdisciplinary contribution), it can be provided in a clearly labeled background section that can be skipped by better informed readers. However, even this strategy entails some sacrifice of precious journal space; thus, such a problem description should only be included under exceptional circumstances. Also, the relevance of the material to the author's results should always be evident to its readers; such background information should never be provided just because the author thought it would be interesting.

Some journal papers report solutions to previously unidentified, sometimes subtle problems. Defining such problems may be such an important step toward their solution that the problem description is actually part of the contribution. But even in this case, the author should indicate that the problem was solved before describing it. First of all, readers will realize that a contribution is being made. Second, some busy journal readers, as implied above, resent efforts to hold their interest by creating suspense.

Incidentally, if an author does choose to begin with a problem description, he or she should be careful that the result is not only a solution to a problem but a solution to the specific problem described. Moreover, if the particular problem can be shown to be only a specific instance of a more general problem, the applicability of its solution in other situations will be more apparent.

*The Statement-of-Objectives Beginning*

An opening somewhat similar to the statement-of-the-problem beginning entails stating—one by one—a list of objectives. This beginning is sometimes used in papers that arise from engineering and programming projects. Later in the introduction, or possibly not until the end of the paper, the author asserts that the first goal was achieved. Moreover, the second objective was attained also, and so forth. Thus, when this opening is used, the reader is taken through the same list of specifications, once as objectives and then as achievements.

The greatest weakness of the statement-of-objectives beginning is that it rarely includes a summarization of the individual achievements, which would enable referees and other readers to identify a specific "bottom line" contribution. The readers themselves are left to do the synthesis. In some cases, this may be because the individual achievements are too unrelated to each other to allow the author to establish the connection. When this is the case and the achievements are not significant enough to be documented in separate shorter papers, there may be no basis for journal publication in the first place.

In papers in which the list-of-objectives opening is used, the corresponding list of achievements often includes overlapping entries of the kind found in promotional brochures. Many journal readers stop reading papers if they think authors are attempting to deceive them about the extent of their contributions.

Users of the statement-of-objectives beginning sometimes defend its use by claiming that the list of goals represents standards by which their actual achievements can be judged. However, such authors may be asking colleagues to judge their achievements on the bases of the authors' criteria, rather than their own. Moreover, claiming the achievement of project goals despite such constraints as limited funds, manpower, and time can sound like a bid for applause; explanations of failures can sound like excuses. In primary journal papers, new results should be compared with the present state of the art. If, in retrospect, an author feels that he or she could have come closer to some of the objectives had a different approach been taken, that should be pointed out in the closing section as a possible direction for further work.

This opening also has the quality of the mystery story. Readers are held in suspense until they learn whether and to what extent each of the goals has been attained. There is always a question of how much attention readers pay to the intervening text before they are given the information they are really waiting for—the exact nature and boundaries of the contribution.

If, despite these perils, the statement-of-objectives opening is used, the author should strive both to summarize the achievements and to fit the contribution into the present state of the art. Moreover, in keeping with the basic philosophy of the journal paper, the author should share the rationale for the objectives with readers if those readers might not be completely sympathetic with them. Finally, the kinds of bulleted lists of achievements that often appear in sales literature should be avoided, especially if the author tries to make one achievement sound like several.

## More Possible Pitfalls

Most of these and possibly other openings can be used successfully if handled skillfully and if chosen on the basis of the particular contribution. In all cases, the introduction should be written as though the reader had no prior knowledge of the contribution. (The title and the abstract should not be implicitly regarded as parts of the introduction, the reason for which is explained in Chapter 5.) However, the reader is assumed to have considerable knowledge of the earlier work on which the new result is based.

The probability of reader frustration will be lower if the transition from knowledge in general to the author's specific contribution is swift (but not so swift that the reader is left bewildered) and if the intervening sentences provide meaningful information to the author's active peers. Moreover, in journal papers, attention should be focused throughout the description of the contribution on the contribution itself, not on later parts of the paper.

Promising opening words for papers that report original contributions include "an algorithm has been devised that. . . ," "semiconductor yield has been increased by. . . ," "a solution has been found to the problem of. . . ," and "a solvent has been formulated that. . . ." However, phrases such as "this paper treats. . . ," "considerations about the design of. . . ," and "we discuss here. . ." rarely identify crisply the nature and extent of new-results.

Authors should also avoid starting journal papers with phrases such as "with the advent of. . . ," "the last decade has seen. . . ," and "a viable alternative to. . . ." The word "paradigm" is rapidly becoming stale among computer scientists. If such weak, overused words and phrases appear at the beginning of a journal paper, readers may conclude that further reading will be equally unrewarding.

## RELATING THE NEW RESULTS TO EXISTING KNOWLEDGE

Regardless of the strategy used to begin, the complete description of an original contribution implies more than the presentation of previously unknown information. As part of that description, the new information must be fitted into the context of present knowledge so that readers can see how it extends and fills gaps in our existing knowledge base. If the comparison can be quantified, readers will be even better able to evaluate the contribution. The new contribution, seen in combination with previously reported results, often reveals possibilities for even further exploration that would not be evident if it were viewed only in isolation. Moreover, the combination may suggest applications not otherwise apparent.

Even within the paper, a complete understanding of the contribution is needed to prepare the reader for the body. Although information intended solely for this purpose should not be included explicitly until the end of introduction (as discussed later), the logical arguments and the experimental evidence provided in the body substantiate the claimed contribution. If the author has been successful in describing that contribution in the introduction, the reader of the body is more likely to understand where that (sometimes difficult) material all leads.

### The Purposes of References

The basic mechanism used to establish the relationship between new information and that presumed to be known by the reader is the citing of references. Although references are discussed more fully in Chapter 6, it is important here that readers be aware of three basic purposes that they serve in journal papers. The most obvious and familiar reason for citing references is to direct readers to further information about a subject, but this use of references is often not as important in papers reporting original results as in some other kinds of technical articles. References also allow the author of a journal paper to build on information that has been established as correct in the formal literature by other investigators. Finally, references help the author to describe claimed new results by fitting them into the framework of previously reported findings.

## The Effective Use of References

Fitting new results into the context of present knowledge is not accomplished simply by citing a cluster of references after the first sentence. It requires that the author, throughout the description of the contribution, carefully integrate the new information into the body of previously reported results, which are assumed to be known by the reader.

Some inexperienced authors think that large numbers of references make a journal paper look scholarly. Actually, too many references that have little bearing on the work reported are a hindrance to the reader in seeing the relationship between the new result and prior art. Long reference lists may be approrpriate in entirely different kinds of articles, such as tutorials and reviews.

## Knowledge of the Literature

New findings cannot be fitted into the fabric of existing knowledge unless the author "knows the literature." In practice, this may not be the case for any of several reasons. An author's discovery may be outside his or her normal area of activity. Such contributions are not unusual from mathematicians, for example, who may have been called upon to solve a problem in another department. (A solution to the same problem may actually have been reported a dozen years before, but in such a way that its applicability in different situations was not apparent.)

Some workers are unfamiliar with the literature because they choose to work in almost complete isolation from their professional colleagues; "reinventing the wheel" is the well-worn phrase used to describe the possible results of this working style.

But the most common reason for lack of knowledge of related work, even by experienced authors, is the emergence of so many new and often overlapping subspecialties and so many new journals to report the results of this work.

### Possible Consequences

The aspiring author who has not kept abreast of related work should do a literature search, examining all papers that might have reported similar results. An author unwilling to undertake this chore early in the project incurs an even greater risk than having the paper rejected. If a referee later points out results so similar to those of the author that publication is unjustified, the author's work, as well as the writing effort, may be wasted. (The use of information retrieval systems at an early stage in the project can reduce the likelihood of this catastrophe.)

An occasional missing reference in papers that report new results in fast-moving disciplines is almost inevitable, even from the papers of well-informed authors. It is in this situation that referees are apt to be helpful, since one of their responsibilities is to ensure the originality of the claimed new result. In the worst case, missing references may indeed lead to rejection of a paper. More often, however, the discovery of a missing reference requires revision of the paper to take the related results into account, but the paper can be salvaged.

*Misuse of Referees*

Although referees do have a responsibility in connection with references, some authors attempt to shift too much of the burden of uncovering related work to referees, who typically perform their essential function voluntarily. We have not only received submissions with no references, occasionally we have even been requested to ask prospective referees to identify related papers for would-be authors. Since the published author is likely ultimately to serve as a referee, perhaps experience will make such authors a little more thoughtful.

**Unfavorable Comparisons with Other Work**

On occasion, in describing their own contributions, authors denigrate the work of fellow investigators. Regardless of what their motives really are, editors and referees are apt to assume that such authors are trying to make their results look good at the expense of others. The actual effect may be the opposite of what these authors intend.

Some inexperienced authors may see their results as an improvement over the present state of the art, and therefore feel justified in being critical of previous work. But this is the nature of progress in science and technology, with new and better results built on what had been known before. Experienced authors usually recognize this fact and are generous in comparing their contributions with prior ones.

A few authors really do attempt to enhance the reception of their papers by attacking the work of others. These tactics are usually more obvious to other researchers than such authors imagine, and they may overlook a very real possibility. Since referees are chosen because they have done similar work, it is not unlikely that the papers of such authors will find their way into the hands of the very people whose work was criticized. Some editors can be expected to arrange matters so that this is exactly what happens.

*Dealing with Defective Related Work*

A final possibility is that the author really does believe that some related work is deficient. An issue of this sort arose some years ago in connection with a submission to us. A previously published paper, cited in the paper under discussion, claimed a result very similar to that reported by the author. One of the referees questioned the need to publish the new paper in view of the previous one. But the author was able to demonstrate that the work in the earlier paper was flawed, although he was unwilling to point out its deficiencies in his own paper. He believed that other workers would ultimately recognize the soundness of his result and the weaknesses in the earlier one.

Not everyone would agree with this author's way of dealing with the problem. Because further work might be based on the defective results, some would contend that the author had a professional obligation to call attention to the problem. Of course, other mechanisms exist for doing this, such as sending a letter to the editor of the journal that published the original paper.

Under these circumstances, most authors would point out the deficiencies in an earlier paper, to avoid the risk of having their own paper rejected because it did not report an original result. Of course, they would be extremely careful to be correct. And they would be as generous as possible, pointing out limitations in the work but never making personal judgments of the author's competence.

## BACKGROUND INFORMATION

It is assumed that the audience for a journal paper is composed of the author's peers, who are supposedly conversant with the literature. Thus, in principle, the introduction should provide very little background information in order not to waste the time of informed readers. But this is completely true only in the most specialized journals and in slowly evolving disciplines. In many areas, significant new results are being reported almost daily from all over the world. Thus, in practice, the author must anticipate the need for background information by readers of the particular paper, possibly including readers working in related specialties. Typically, the audience for a single paper is much smaller than for the journal in which it appears. In general, therefore, an author is unwise not to provide a modest amount of background information if it can significantly increase the size of the audience without unduly penalizing more active peers. Of course, we do not mean to encourage the wordy presentations of background information, well known even to informed laymen, that sometimes bloat submitted manuscripts. But just how far the author should go is a difficult question to answer. Some classification may make this problem more tractable.

### Kinds of Background Information

There are two broad classes of background information: that needed to understand material provided in the body of the paper, after the introduction; that needed to help the reader to understand the character of the contribution. The former kind of information (mathematical notation is an example) should not be provided until after the introduction. Such information is not relevant for readers who want to learn about the contribution, many of whom will not go beyond the introduction anyhow. Thus, we defer further consideration of this class of background information until later chapters.

## Factual Information

Information needed by at least some readers to understand the character of the contribution may include, as a subclass, detailed factual information. Facts are less likely to be remembered than conceptual information. For example, readers are not likely to recall numbers gathered in an earlier study by a psychologist that may be needed to understand a new result. If a modest amount of such data are required, the author can simply provide them again (being sure to give credit to their originator).

Problems arise as the amount of factual background information grows. Because it may be difficult for some readers to acquire an earlier paper, authors should seek alternatives to that. Perhaps the needed data can be reproduced in a table or an appendix, separated from the running text so that readers who do not need it can easily skip it. Because the original paper was copyrighted, the author must obtain permission in writing from the editor of the journal in which it appeared in order to reproduce it.

But if much previously published data are required, a point is reached where there may be no realistic alternative to the reader having the original paper in hand as the current one is read. (The author of the original paper, whose professional affiliation should have appeared in the journal in which the paper was published, is probably equipped to satisfy a request for a reprint.)

## Conceptual Information

Journal readers are much more likely to remember conceptual background information, and we are less sympathetic about repeating it in the current paper. To do so tends to dilute the primary journal paper, which ought to reward its readers' efforts with new information. However, there are few absolute rules in the writing of journal papers. Thus, a difficult question that concerns authors, editors, and referees is the extent to which journal papers ought to cater to the needs of readers who are not completely conversant with the literature. Students are often in this category and may encounter significant barriers in getting started reading journal papers. (It is assumed in the current paper that the reader is familiar with the literature cited in it; the authors of the referenced papers, in turn, assumed that their readers were familiar with the literature cited in them; and so on.) Although the needs of such readers should usually be satisfied by other kinds of articles (tutorials, reviews, and so forth), it may sometimes be more efficient for journal papers to provide background information that is highly relevant for understanding the contribution reported. If the author does decide to provide such information, it should be written as tersely as possible.

### Audience Requirements for Background Information

The most important consideration in determining the amount and kind of background information to provide, of course, is the intended audience for the particular paper, as opposed to the larger audience for the journal in which it is to appear. In some cases, there may be no alternative to providing a considerable amount of such information, because it does not exist in a form suitable for the expected readers of the paper.

We recall a typical real-life situation. A new method had been devised for encoding digital data that are to be recorded on magnetic storage media. This contribution had been documented in an esoteric paper that required considerable mathematical sophistication on the part of the reader. Later, a significant application of this method was developed, and an engineering paper was prepared to document this advance in the state of the art. However, only a small percentage of the audience for the second paper could be expected to understand the original one.

An understanding of the structure of journal papers made the chore a little easier for the author of the engineering paper. The original paper not only described the new coding scheme, it demonstrated its mathematical validity. The author of the current paper did not have to repeat the proof; that was already part of the formal literature. Instead, the author of the engineering paper had to demonstrate the feasibility of applying the scheme in practice, so that readers could duplicate the application. Of course, the author of the new paper gave appropriate credit to the originator of the technique.

### Isolating Background Information

If the audience for a paper is divided between those who need a reasonable amount of conceptual background information and those who would be inconvenienced by it, there is a way in which the author can have the best of both worlds. After alerting readers about what to expect, the background information can be provided in a clearly labeled passage that can be skipped by those not needing it. We are thinking here in terms of paragraphs, though, not pages.

### SIGNIFICANCE OF THE WORK

We alluded to significance early in this chapter and indicated concern that discussions of significance could introduce confusion into descriptions of contributions. There are indeed questions about where in the journal paper significance ought to be discussed. Moreover, although referees are asked to assess significance, there may even be a question of whether it ought to be discussed explicitly at all in journal papers.

Whether significance is dealt with, as such, may depend on the definition of significance and the nature of the contribution; it may also depend on the interests of people other than the author and the author's peers. Ultimately the decision must be an individual one, with the prospective author making a trade-off among a number of factors. If significance is treated explicitly, where in the paper it is handled and how it is dealt with must also be considered.

## Measures of Significance

To the scientist engaged in basic research, significance is measured in terms of how far understanding is advanced by a particular discovery, with new knowledge being valued for its own sake. Thus, some new findings are seen to advance knowledge only in small increments; but, occasionally, a new result may represent a major leap in understanding, with the meaning of many previously unexplained observations suddenly becoming clear. Significance in this sense is usually communicated to journal readers by the description of the contribution itself, including its relationship to previously reported results, and its appreciation relies on the reader's extensive knowledge in the area of the contribution. If the author has done a good job of describing the contribution in the introduction, usually nothing else is required to equip his or her peers to understand its significance.

Occasionally, however, a scientist may indicate in the introduction subtle implications of the new information to the discipline if they are not likely to occur to his or her peers. Recognition of the importance of some new results may be needlessly delayed because authors failed to provide a small amount of such information. However, the author must carefully avoid belaboring what is obvious to the reader. Moreover, for an audience using such a basic measure of significance, the author should be especially wary of appealing to more practical and popular measures of significance.

The significance of less specialized and more practical contributions—those of the applied scientist and the engineer, for example—can often be appreciated to some extent even by readers having less specialized knowledge than the author. For instance, an improvement of 5 percent in how efficiently electric motors use energy is more significant than an improvement of only 2 percent. However, a full appreciation of the significance of such contributions is still only possible by the author's peers. Their knowledge of the field enables them to understand the difficulties that the author had to overcome in obtaining the results and the opportunities that the contribution, in combination with other knowledge in the discipline, opens for even further discoveries.

Again, the author usually need do little beyond writing a good introduction to communicate the significance of such contributions to colleagues. But in this case, too, all of the implications of some new results may not have occurred even to them. Thus, the author might discuss subtle implications of new results for peers and also for those working in related disciplines (readers we call *near peers*). As long as the discussion is not tedious for workers active in the specialty, these less theoretically oriented readers are likely to be tolerant of more popular and practical measures of significance.

Up to this point, we have been considering significance primarily as it is perceived by the author's peers. However, it may be both desirable and possible to communicate in a journal paper some appreciation of the implications of new results to wider audiences, including science reporters, informed laymen, and even the public in general.

A fundamental problem in treating the broader implications of new results in journal papers is that, as the audience gets larger, more readers will use different measures of significance from those used by the author's peers. For example, some contributions may have dramatic commercial or social implications but may be regarded as trivial achievements by members of the author's discipline. It would be unfortunate if the author with a modest contribution in the view of colleagues appeared to be appealing to a larger audience that used more popular measures of significance. Moreover, there is an added writing problem with discussions of this kind of significance: They are directed at a different audience from the rest of the paper, requiring a more labored writing style that could be tiresome for the author's peers.

These problems may account for the strong belief of some journal authors that getting and reporting their results to their peers ends their obligation and that it is someone else's job to consider the wider implications of their discoveries for other readers. However, the question of whether to indicate broader significance to a larger audience is often more complicated than that, with several individuals and groups having a stake in the decision. Indeed, in some cases, the author may have little choice in the matter.

## Interested Parties

Sometimes the *author* may want to communicate the broader implications of his or her discoveries to a wider audience. After all, most of us would like more people to admire our achievements. If it is done tastefully, the peers of some authors may be tolerant of a brief discussion of significance for a less well-informed audience.

The *author's peers* are investing valuable time and energy in reading the paper. These readers constitute the primary audience; they are the ones most likely to use the new information as a stepping stone to further discoveries; and, in the long run, they are also the readers whose opinion is most important to the author. Nothing should be done hastily that could interfere with satisfying their needs.

The author's *near peers* are a little less likely to recognize all of the implications of a new result. After all, they have not been thinking for months or years about the work as have the author and his or her active peers. The results of research and development may be more fully exploited if its significance can be communicated to near peers. Discussing significance for these readers may actually be instrumental in winning far wider recognition for the author and even for the discipline.

The *sponsors* of research may have a legitimate concern about the treatment in journal papers of the significance of new results for more general audiences. In some cases, an understood requirement may govern how the broader significance of a researcher's results is handled. For example, we have been told that some authors are expected to include material in the introductions of their journal papers that can easily be excerpted by a public relations department to provide the basis for a press release or even to be used directly by the news media.

The *science reporter,* the *informed layman,* and even the *public* may have a right to be told about the significance of the results of research. Many new discoveries do profoundly affect our lives, and public funds may even have supported the research. Discussions of significance in journal papers would rarely be aimed at the general public. However, science reporters and informed laymen, who can be assumed to have some training in the discipline, may read journal paper introductions. Since the author is obviously the best-qualified person to discuss the broader significance of the results, it may be in his or her best interest to do so, to avoid misunderstandings. For example, responsible authors of medical papers might prevent exaggerated expectations by the public if they included carefully written discussions of significance.

**Treating Significance in the Journal Paper**

If the author chooses to or must treat the implications of the discovery explicitly (and if the contribution is such that it is practical to do so), he or she must decide the level of knowledge the audience is assumed to have. If the audience includes readers who are not active workers in the specialty, the author must be especially careful not to forget the primary audience and its possible reaction to the passage. In Chapter 1, we claimed that scientific rigor was the most important of three characteristics that we associated with the primary journal paper. (In addition to our comments there, we touch upon this intriguing topic in later chapters as well.) Yet, in our experience, authors are more likely to forget about scientific rigor when discussing significance than in any other part of the paper. For example, if an author designed an automobile engine having a combustion chamber that used gasoline more efficiently, speculation about the number of barrels of imported oil that would be saved each year might be included. This kind of extrapolation is often based on data of questionable reliability (not usually shared with the reader in any case) and typically involves tacit assumptions.

If the implications of new results are included in journal papers, they must be plausible to the author's peers, even if they are intended for a different audience. Authors who seem unable to discern between "hype" and scientific arguments can arouse doubts about other aspects of their work in the minds of their readers. Moreover, because claims made about significance are more likely to be accepted if the author has an established reputation, the beginning author must be especially prudent. (Our use of the word "intriguing" in the last paragraph was deliberate. This topic does indeed intrigue us, but we have no right to assume that it intrigues everybody. Authors of journal papers are generally not free to use adjectives as loosely as we did, even when discussing significance for nonpeers.)

When opinions about the significance of new results are included, it must also be made clear to the reader that the author knows that opinions are being expressed. Even then, the author should be modest and restrained; after all, one is discussing the importance of one's own achievements. Moreover, an accurate portrayal of significance requires that limitations as well as advantages be discussed frankly. Authors who culminate glowing descriptions of the significance of their discoveries by mentioning a single innocuous shortcoming do not deceive all journal readers.

## Choosing Where to Treat Significance

If information about significance is explicitly included in the introduction for an audience of peers and near peers, it can usually be provided at the end of the description of the contribution, after readers have gained some understanding of the character of the discovery and its relationship to previous results. Thus, readers are better equipped to appreciate significance. (It should be noted that subtle implications of new results for peers and near peers might already have been suggested in the title and the abstract, and more elaborate discussion will probably be included in the closing section. The treatment of significance in other parts of the paper is discussed in Chapter 5.)

Discussions of the broader implications of new results for audiences that include readers who are neither peers nor near peers should be clearly separated from other kinds of information. As indicated earlier, the mixing of motives for providing information can always lead to reader confusion.

But beyond that, such discussions have to be written differently because they have a different audience.

Opinions vary about where in the paper to treat significance for wider audiences. One recommendation that we have heard is to postpone it until the closing section. Advocates of this approach feel that by then the author has earned the right to speculate a little, by the scholarliness of the presentation and the mastery of the subject evident throughout earlier parts of the paper (the author's credentials have been established). Moreover, readers of the concluding section are presumed to be armed with the scientific information provided in the body and are thus better equipped to appreciate significance.

Although it is often desirable to discuss significance for the benefit of peers and even near peers in closings (as suggested in Chapter 5), we think that, if such discussions for wider audiences were postponed until then, they would probably be missed by the many readers of introductions who do not read more of the paper. Besides, discussions of significance in closings are intended to serve a different purpose—to motivate further work by the author's peers. Thus, we think that, if discussions of significance for broader audiences are included anywhere, they too should be provided in a separate passage within the introduction.

## HINTS AT APPROACHES

When describing the contribution in the introduction, the journal author may also include a limited amount of general information suggesting the approach that was taken. For example, phrases may be used such as "experiments were conducted to. . . ," "we devised an algorithm that. . . ," and so on. Suggestive words such as "analytical" and "statistical" may be used. These enable the paper to be characterized somewhat for the reader, and the author can indicate, for example, that an unconventional technique was used to gather data. However, except in methodology papers (where the contribution is the method), authors should not dilute the main purpose of the introduction with much information about how they obtained their results. It is the job of the body to supply that kind of information.

## PREVIEWING THE REST OF THE PAPER

Authors often preview the general structure and contents of the remainder of the paper at the end of the introduction. Especially in rather long, complexly organized papers, most readers feel uncomfortable if they do not know beforehand where they are being led, and this information can provide badly needed orientation. The preview is helpful also in providing motivation to read the rest of the paper. This passage can be made even more meaningful if a little attention is given to the rationale for the choice and ordering of topics.

Placing this information at the end of the introduction puts it immediately before the material in the body to which it applies. Moreover, the many readers of the introduction who do not read the body can simply stop reading when they reach this passage, without missing information relevant for them. We think it is a mistake to put this preview in the first paragraph of the introduction or even in the abstract, as is sometimes done.

## THE ACTUAL WRITING

Many authors defer writing introductions until they have written the rest of the paper. As indicated at the beginning of this chapter, the introduction is sometimes regarded as the most difficult part of the paper to write. Although success is the only meaningful measure of the effectiveness of individual approaches to writing, we think that writing the introduction first coincides with the seemingly natural progression of going from the general to the specific (from the outside to the inside). We also believe that the act of writing the introduction further crystallizes the author's thinking about the exact nature of the contribution, which can influence the way the other parts of the paper are written. Specifically, the relevance of some of the theoretical and experimental material provided in the body depends on the new results that the author has claimed in the introduction. Of course, if later the author is not satisfied, at any time during or after writing the rest of the paper, further refinements can be made; in practice, the introduction may sometimes have to be rewritten completely.

### The Use of Complex Sentence Structure

Despite the great care required of authors to make general statements that are at the same time correct, the kind of information provided in the introduction is often easily assimilated by readers. Thus, the author should avoid simple declarative sentences in the introduction, which might be appropriate, say, in describing a complicated step-by-step procedure. This near-mathematical style in an introduction can create considerable impatience in readers. Instead, complex sentences with subordinate clauses and phrases provide more ideas per page for the busy journal reader. Moreover, communicating ideas in complex sentences establishes relationships more effectively than presenting the same ideas separately, and it is just such relationships that are needed in the introduction to establish the "big picture."

## SUMMARY

In this chapter, the introduction to the primary journal paper was treated. We believe this to be the most important part of the paper, and also the most difficult part to write. The need for explicit identification of original contributions was stressed; some possible reasons for failing to do so were suggested; and four ways of beginning were discussed. We generally favored opening with a description of the contribution, but we supported use of the statement-of-the-problem beginning for papers reporting solutions both to classical and to previously unidentified problems. Historical openings were generally believed to be more suitable for articles aimed at nonspecialists, although they might be used for interdisciplinary papers or in areas of investigation that have long been dormant. We were not enthusiastic about the statement-of-objectives beginning either, but we advised authors who do choose to use it to summarize their results so that readers can identify a specific contribution.

Fitting new results into the context of present knowledge was said not only to define the bounds of the new contribution, but also to reveal further research and application opportunities. Establishing the relationships between a new result and prior knowledge was said to be one of three purposes that references serve in journal papers. However, the inexperienced author was cautioned against making unflattering comparisons with previously published work.

We sympathized with the difficult problems that authors face in determining how much background information to provide, as well as the most appropriate place to provide it. We suggested that background information needed to understand the body be excluded from the introduction. We proposed classification of other background information, as a means of helping the author to deal with it. A careful assessment of reader requirements was felt to be the most crucial consideration in determining the amount and kind of background information to provide.

Discussions of the significance of authors' discoveries were then considered, and two different measures of importance were identified: that used by the author's peers and possibly near peers, and that used by larger audiences. Despite the opinion of some experienced authors that significance as measured by nonpeers not be considered at all in journal papers, or be treated only in concluding sections, an author might want or be obliged to include such material in the introduction. If so, we cautioned authors not to forget completely about the sensibilities of their peers.

Hints might be given in the introduction about the approach used in obtaining new results, but it was suggested that most of this information be withheld until later in the paper.

We urged authors to follow the practice of including a preview of the rest of the paper at the end of the introduction to help establish and maintain reader orientation.

In the actual writing of the introduction, we contradicted the advice often given about all technical writing—to use simple declarative sentences. Instead, we recommended the use of complex sentence structure so as to provide at a faster pace information that can be easily understood.

Thus, the introduction to a typical journal paper might begin with a clear identification of the contribution. A few sentences might be needed before this statement to set the stage, and a few paragraphs or a few pages might be required after it to fully describe the character and limits of the author's result and to fit it into the context of existing knowledge. Background information needed by a significant percentage of readers to understand the contribution might then be included in a labeled subsection that could be skipped by readers not requiring it, but background information needed only to understand the body of the paper would usually be omitted from the introduction. The author might then discuss (with suitable modesty) the significance of the results for an audience that even included readers other than peers and near peers. Some hints might also be included about the approach used in getting the new results. The introduction would probably end with a textual outline of the rest of the paper.

In our experience, the most common weaknesses in the introductions to journal papers are failure to claim a specific contribution, failure to fit the contribution into the current state of the art, and inclusion of details that should have been withheld for the body. Appendix A provides a checklist to be used in measuring the effectiveness of introductions.

# 3

# *Theoretical Material*

Some technical articles, if they deal with an original contribution at all, describe only a result and provide little or no insight into how it was achieved. The bodies of these "black box" articles are simply elaborations of the claims made in their introductions. But in a journal paper, it is the material in the body that most clearly distinguishes it from other technical literature, for it is here that the author describes the logical justification and the experimentation on which the findings are based. Indeed, without this information the reader cannot be sure that the author has anything to contribute.

Present-day researchers have several advantages over those of even a few generations ago. In addition to beginning from an immense knowledge base, there is better understanding of the scientific method and its implications for arriving at correct conclusions. Progress continues in areas such as the philosophy of science, cognitive science, and even artificial intelligence, with ever deepening understanding of the processes involved in human reasoning. Nonetheless, many authors of journal papers have had limited exposure to these ideas. The heavy educational demands on the researcher tend to exclude subject matter not directly related to his or her chosen specialty. But all researchers apply these principles, and they are reflected in the descriptions of their mental activities in the bodies of journal papers. (Books on epistemology and the philosophy of science are identified in the Notes at the back of the book.[18-21] Ongoing work in this area is reported in, for example, issues of *The British Journal for the Philosophy of Science*. Efforts to imitate these human processes in computers are described in papers appearing in such publications as *Artificial Intelligence* and the *Journal of Automated Reasoning*.)

Because considerable concentration may be required to understand the body of a journal paper, those readers who choose to do so can be assumed to have a deeper interest in the author's findings than do those who are content merely to accept the claims made earlier in the paper. Readers of the body may themselves be doing similar research; they may plan to use or to extend the author's results; or they may even be skeptical about the claims of the author. Such readers are not just passive receptors of facts, who are satisfied with the general idea. They must be able to follow the author's reasoning exactly to assure themselves of the validity of the claims. On the other hand, writing the body confronts the author with many opportunities to lose the reader in a morass of complicated mathematics or in convoluted chains of reasoning. It is only awareness of such possibilities by the author that reduces the likelihood of their occurrence.

We discuss in this chapter some of the problems faced by authors in presenting one kind of information that may appear in the body of a journal paper—theoretical developments. Experimental confirmation as well as theoretical justification is often needed to establish the correctness of new knowledge, and we consider the presentation of that kind of information in the next chapter. However, much of what is said here is applicable in presenting that kind of material also, especially when one considers the complex reasoning often involved in extracting information from experimental data.

We regard theoretical passages to be those involving the development of often complex mathematical and logical constructs. Mathematics, computer science, and the engineering disciplines have given rise to a great deal of such material. An extension to theoretical knowledge in the physical sciences, such as a more complete understanding of a natural phenomenon, may actually be reported in what we refer to as an experimental paper, if its validity is confirmed by a series of experiments, rather than primarily by logical and mathematical developments.

## THEORETICAL CONSTRUCTS

If readers of a journal paper were to agree with a few basic assumptions made by an author, the author could manipulate these statements in ways acceptable to all readers capable of understanding the manipulations and could arrive at conclusions with which all such readers would agree. In essence, this is exactly how journal authors attempt to establish the logical validity of their claims. However, this simple notion can become extremely complex in practice. The words in the author's statements are actually symbols representing objects and interactions and dependencies among the objects. But as the number of objects increases and as the relationships among them become more complicated, expressing them in everyday language can become too cumbersome and imprecise to be practical. Thus, the words in the author's sentences may themselves have to be represented by other symbols, the meanings of which must be communicated to readers. Moreover, the manipulations may become so complex that advanced mathematics is needed to carry them out. Of course, the journal author is not required to teach the mathematics to readers except in papers that extend mathematical theory itself. But the author does have to carefully and patiently lead them through the applications of it so that they can see for themselves the soundness of the theoretical arguments.

In our attempts to understand how best to write theoretical material in journal papers, we have identified four kinds of information that may be required to enable readers to evaluate the validity of the assertions made earlier in the paper: (1) the contentions to be proved; (2) the underlying assumptions and their rationale; (3) essential factual information (such as mathematical notation and definitions of special terms); and (4) the theoretical developments themselves. A fifth kind of information may be included also: (5) logical arguments intended to persuade readers of the applicability of the theory when experimental information is limited or absent.

It is not essential for authors to determine whether particular required information should go into one or another of these categories; but, because they encompass everything that might be needed, they can be helpful in identifying the information needs of readers. It should be noted also that the order in which these kinds of information are discussed here is not necessarily the same as the order that they are provided in journal papers; indeed, more than one category of information is often provided in the same sentence.

We begin by discussing two topics that must concern authors throughout the theoretical portions of their papers: the organization of theoretical material, and the relevance of information included in theoretical passages. We then examine each of the five kinds of information in detail. Afterwards, we suggest an informal test using reader-colleagues to measure success in communicating the theory. In the final section, we note a common reason for the rejection of predominantly theoretical papers. Appendix B at the end of the book is a checklist to help authors to measure the success of their theoretical passages.

## ORGANIZING THEORETICAL MATERIAL

The purpose of a theoretical passage is to demonstrate the logical basis for the author's claims, and the purpose of organization is to facilitate comprehension of this information. Organization need not parallel the original groping of the author in the search for answers. In retrospect, that can often be seen to have been needlessly indirect. Instead, the author should seek a beautifully straightforward organization, where there is greater likelihood that readers will be able to see the soundness of the reasoning.

If there seems to be no single best organization for a given passage, all other things being equal, the simpler of two approaches is usually preferable. Readers may already be struggling with difficult material and should not have to cope also with organizational complexity.

## The Rationale for the Organization

With increasing organizational complexity, it becomes increasingly important that readers be told about the organization beforehand. Reader orientation may be helped even further if the author also suggests the rationale for the approach. For example, we implied above that we would discuss organization and the relevance of information first in this chapter, because these concerns prevail throughout theoretical passages.

## Hierarchical Structure

If readers of theoretical material are given great quantities of details, but with long delays before they are told how the details are related to each other or to higher level concepts, they are at least apt to become impatient. If they are never given more than the details, serious errors are likely as they attempt to establish the relationships among the details themselves. The preferred alternative is to begin at the most general level and to proceed in easy steps downward to the details. A single criterion should be sought for partitioning the grand strategy into, say, seven or fewer topics, each requiring greater elaboration.[22] All information provided at the most general level must apply to at least two topics, with details peculiar to a single topic that is to be expanded later omitted. Afterward, each topic can be developed further separately, probably with a brief introduction reminding readers of its relationship to information provided at the next higher level. As the intervening space between the higher level discussion and the treatment of an individual topic increases, such reminders become more important.

If any of the separate topics requires further breakdown, that can be handled similarly. However, if more than one criterion is used as the basis for dividing subject matter at any particular level, reader confusion is likely.

If there are too many or too few divisions at each level or if the places where divisions are made are too unnatural, comprehension may also be a problem. For example, an author submitted a paper to us that was divided into exactly 50 coordinate sections. Later, the work reported proved to be an important contribution to mathematics, but few of the author's peers could have been expected to grasp how 50 separate pieces are related to each other. Dividing subject matter into too few pieces at each level can also cause problems. The confusion in this case results from each topic being introduced too many times with too little additional information provided at each level.

## Further Support of the Organization

The expository strategy outlined above can sometimes be enhanced by the running example, in which a skeletal illustrative case is fleshed out in parallel with the description, with each reinforcing the other as the author's logic unfolds.

The communication of many hierarchical structures can also be reinforced by suitably designed illustrations. Note that such figures are often just as effective for representing abstract concepts as physical equipment or systems.[23]

## Top-Down Design

The hierarchical approach to organization outlined above, long familiar to writers, was discovered a decade or so ago by computer programmers, who refer to it as "top-down design." Indeed, one benefit claimed for this programming strategy is that it helps human beings to understand computer programs.

## The Bottom-Up Alternative

Some authors attempt a bottom-up approach to organizing theoretical material. Here the author prepares an outline that is in fact a list of topics. Then, a separate passage is written for each topic. However, despite later attempts to incorporate transitional material (which some authors do not even make), the result is likely to be badly fragmented, with the reader hard pressed to integrate the pieces into a coherent whole. Communication of complex material seems to require that the author have a completely integrated high-level view of the material and that he or she begin by passing that view on to the reader.

## The Limitations of Organization

Despite its unquestioned importance, the significance of organization is sometimes overestimated. Many reviewers of technical papers automatically recommend that unduly difficult-to-follow technical material be reorganized, when in actuality the problem can often be corrected by other means, such as the addition of introductory and orienting information or the excising of extraneous information. And no organization can overcome the omission of needed facts or the lack of care in expressing difficult ideas unambiguously.

## EXCLUDING CURRENTLY IRRELEVANT INFORMATION

There is an added reason for omitting superfluous information from theoretical passages, beyond the journal author's usual concern with efficient communication: Readers cannot be confused by needless information if it is not present in the first place. Moreover, withholding information not currently essential to understanding can often ease the passage of readers through the complexities of logical and mathematical material.

For example, as implied in discussing organization, all of the author's logical processes need not be reported in an autobiographical way. The purpose is to communicate as clearly as possible the logicality of the author's conclusions, not to provide a diary of personal experiences. Occasionally, an unproductive approach that the author considered might be mentioned briefly if readers are likely to think that it was overlooked. However, the discussion of alternatives should usually be deferred until readers have worked their way through the actual mathematical or logical developments.

Another source of confusion in theoretical material is the parenthetical observations that some authors think might interest their readers. Even when such commentary is put in footnotes, many readers are likely to suspend their reading (and their concentration) to examine the footnotes.

Moreover, readers of journal papers should never be given information for no better reason than that the author knows it. Many inexperienced authors are unable to resist this temptation, but such material can become a "red herring" and is especially irritating to readers who are already grappling with difficult theoretical material.

We recall a submission that appeared to have good potential for publication if it were suitably revised. The revision arrived with two lengthy but well known derivations incorporated that had not been in the original paper. The authors' explanation for including this irrelevant "window dressing" was that the original manuscript did not seem to be "technical" enough for a journal. However, readers of journal papers expect to be rewarded for their reading effort with significant original results, especially for working their way through mathematics.

Throughout the remainder of this chapter, we note other instances of irrelevant information, as well as cases in which the presentation of some information might better be withheld until a more appropriate time.

## STATING THE CONTENTIONS TO BE PROVED

One of the most frequently overlooked obligations of authors of theoretical material is the need to communicate exactly what they are attempting to prove. If the reader understands fully the character of the contribution as it was described in the introduction, he or she is better equipped to understand the theoretical developments leading to it, at least on a global level. Applying the same principle on the local level—that is, letting the reader know beforehand what is to be shown next—can be immensely helpful within theoretical passages also. In some papers, the reader is instead plunged directly into, what are for him or her, totally meaningless mathematical developments. The defense offered by some authors is that their readers will be able to follow their mathematics. However, they overlook entirely the need for readers to know what purpose the mathematics is serving and, moreover, to know it before they are given the mathematics.

## Keeping the Reader Oriented

As well as introducing theoretical and mathematical arguments with clear statements of purpose, to keep readers oriented, the author can also from time to time sum up what has been demonstrated so far, remind readers of its relationship to higher level strategy, and explain what is to be shown next. Thus, journal readers need to know what the author is attempting to prove as well as the organization of the presentation being used to prove it.

## A Limit on Terseness

The desire to write journal papers tersely was emphasized in Chapter 1, but this goal should never be used to justify the omission of essential orienting information, without which readership is pointlessly reduced. Of course, this approach can be carried to such extremes that some readers become bored. Nonetheless, a little risk in this direction seems to be worth taking, because, if readers are not able to understand the theoretical material provided in the body, this segment of the audience, presumably composed of those readers most interested in the new results, will be lost to the author.

In practice, some authors find it useful to spell out just what they are doing in almost painful detail to be sure that their readers can follow everything. Afterward, they revise the material so as to provide the same information, but in the least amount of space possible.

## IDENTIFYING UNDERLYING ASSUMPTIONS

In theoretical passages, logical and mathematical analyses often represent the author's attempts to understand actual phenomena. Although the scientific method requires that the correspondence between a theoretical or mathematical model and reality ultimately be demonstrated by experimentation, the two come together at other points as well. Indeed, a significant part of the writing effort in many theoretical passages is expended to establish such relationships. One of the most important examples is in communicating the premises or assumptions on which the logic and mathematics are based. Readers must also be convinced that the author's assumptions are realistic. If their justification is not generally accepted in the discipline, it too must be provided. (Even the author may discover flaws through greater awareness of the assumptions on which the logic is founded.)

## Making Assumptions Explicit

The assumptions underlying the logic in journal papers are not necessarily obvious parallels to simple syllogisms, and it may not be possible merely to list them. They may reflect the author's view of the way complex natural processes occur or complicated equipment functions. Thus, intricate networks of assumptions may be involved, which may have to be identified and justified throughout the theoretical passage. For example, a model intended to predict the behavior of the national economy would be based on the author's assumptions regarding an extraordinarily complex system of causes and effects. Such models are significantly simplified representations of actual phenomena. The problem is compounded in this case because the models used for such applications deal only with probable, rather than mathematically exact, relationships among events. If the author's assumptions about these relationships are not correct, the "econometric" model would not be a sound base to be extended by other investigators nor to be used to predict the economic future.

In practice, papers dealing with such models often report only extensions and refinements of them, and many of the assumptions on which the models are based are generally accepted by the author's peers. However, if a hypothetical example is assumed in which a basically different view of the economy (or some other phenomenon) is taken, the author has additional obligations. In order for the testing implicit in journal publication to occur, this author's complete description of the modeled activity, including basic assumptions and their justification, must be provided so that the reader can evaluate the contribution.

It should be noted that this author's model may already have been characterized briefly in the introduction to acquaint readers with the contribution; a more definitive description may have to be provided in the body to enable readers to assure themselves that the model corresponds with reality.

## Some Justifiable Repetition

We have encountered authors who have been concerned that describing the same model twice is not consistent with the efficient communication desired in journal papers. However, the treatment of the model in the introduction served a different purpose—to make claims about its capabilities. The description in the body explains and justifies the assumptions on which the model is based, as well as providing its mathematical or logical structure. Indeed, it is the failure of some kinds of technical articles to provide this latter information in the body that was alluded to in the first paragraph of this chapter (the black box article).

On the other hand, had the fuller description been provided in the introduction, efficiency would have been reduced. The many readers of the introduction who do not read the body would not be rewarded for the extra effort needed to understand the more complete description. Moreover, providing a second, more elaborate description in the body has didactic value.

It is akin to the top-down organization mentioned earlier (and to a journalistic technique discussed in Chapter 5). Readers of the body, because of their previous exposure to the model's properties in the introduction, are better equipped to understand the more definitive description.

## Staying in Touch with Reality

We make much of the issue of assumptions and other relationships between models and reality because they are often not well established in journal submissions. In some cases, the mathematics seems so beautifully logical to the author that it is hard for him or her to believe that it does not correspond with the phenomenon being modeled. Indeed, some authors convey the impression that if an activity does not correspond with their model, it certainly ought to! The penchant of theoreticians to thoughtlessly equate their models with the real activities they imitate is often evident, even in conversation. The mathematical analog for them becomes the reality. One of many examples is the computer scientist who calls a matrix of numbers, representing the light intensities needed to generate a display on a graphics device, an "image."

## Methodology Papers

Readers of this book will probably have seen descriptions of some kinds of mathematical models in journal papers in which little attention was given to assumptions and no experimental evidence was provided to demonstrate their correspondence with reality. Despite what we have said so far, there may be justification for publishing such papers. For example, a novel and mathematically interesting modeling technique might be reported that would be of great value to other workers. For instance, such a paper might report a basic extension to queueing theory. However, the contribution here is the methodology, and only its mathematical properties are of concern.

## PROVIDING OTHER NEEDED FACTS

We think that journal readers, especially those who are sufficiently interested to read the theoretical material in the body, attempt to understand everything as they read. If they encounter even a few obstacles to understanding, they stop reading, rather than gloss over occasional uncertainties. But failure to include all facts essential to understanding is, in our experience, the most common weakness in the theoretical portions of submitted manuscripts.

Even though the reader knows what the author is trying to prove and has been provided with enough of the assumptions and their justification to proceed, other facts are often needed before and during the time the reader works through the author's logical developments. Mathematical and theoretical passages often include sentences and sentence fragments to state propositions and theorems, to provide definitions, to explain proofs, to define notation, and to make observations—any of which may include facts without which the reader cannot proceed. Information that is sometimes found in introductions (such as mathematical notation), but which we suggested be omitted from there in journal papers, also falls into this category.

In more formal material, the missing information may be as mundane as the significance of some mathematical notation or a basic definition. In less formal material, however, it might be a more subtle fact about which the reader cannot know unless he has been told. We recently read a manuscript that reported an image processing technique intended for applications in medical diagnosis. Photographs of displays of ventricles were presented to demonstrate the effectiveness of the method. However, in the original version of the paper, the author forgot to indicate whether the ventricles in this experimental material were in the heart or the brain.

### Specialized Facts

In identifying required facts, authors must be even more careful about specialized information than that typically obtainable in the literature or from other sources. If previously published information is not known, some of the audience may be lost, but at least the information can be obtained by determined readers. But efforts to find information directly related to the work may be fruitless. For example, a description of a method for controlling the flow of work in a large computer system might require some specialized knowledge not easily obtained by the average reader. In the particular system, for instance, jobs expected to take less than some predetermined amount of computer time might automatically be given priority over longer running jobs.

(In general, the description of such a scheduling method ought to be written so as to require as little knowledge of the particular system as possible. The more abstract description enables readers to more easily see applicability of the technique in different settings, and it is less likely to contain distracting information peculiar to the particular implementation but of no value to readers attempting to discover transferable concepts.)

### Treatment of Needed Facts

Comprehension of theoretical material may be affected by the placement and handling of required facts. For example, such information may be needed to understand all or large parts of theoretical passages, or it may be needed only locally. It may be self-contained, or there may be no context to aid readers in remembering it. Two obvious principles can be applied in treating such information: Authors can withhold factual information until it is actually required; and they can also attempt to provide facts in context, both done to reduce the need for memorization. (Obviously, such information should never be withheld until after it is needed, as some authors do.)

We use mathematical notation here as an example of the kind of facts with which we are concerned; it may or may not form a self-contained body of information, it may apply broadly or it may be needed only locally, and it is a kind of information with which journal authors commonly must contend. Definitions of special terms and basic concepts might be treated similarly.

## Systems of Notation

Self-contained systems of notation have been devised to represent a wide variety of logical relationships ranging from chemical reactions to the syntax of programming languages,[24] and it is not unusual for authors to devise such systems for temporary use in communicating theory in an individual paper. For example, an author might define a special set of symbols for use in describing the activities occurring within automatic transmissions for automobiles. This kind of information often forms its own context and can usually be placed near the beginning of the passage in which it will be used. Of course, motivation should still be provided; even when a context exists, readers should know why they are being asked to master such material.

## Mathematical Symbol Definitions

There is often so little context in a list of mathematical symbols and their definitions, however, that remembering them is akin to memorizing nonsense syllables. It is for this reason that we do not recommend the practice of providing a glossary of mathematical symbols—not just at the beginning of the body, but at the beginning of the paper. This information must either be memorized or skipped until it is needed. We think that most journal readers tend to read everything as they encounter it, but going through this notation long before it is needed may be largely wasted effort.

Providing other factual information before theoretical passages, rather than integrating it into them, is often done for the convenience of the author, rather than to help the reader. The author can feel that the obligation of providing the information has been fulfilled. However, the reader may have to search backwards through the paper to remind himself of facts provided earlier in order to understand concepts currently being presented.

If, instead, each definition or other fact is provided at the point of its first use—near an equation, for example—a context exists that facilitates memorization. For example, symbol definitions may be listed after the equation, or the association between symbols and objects can be established in the text immediately surrounding the equation. Some authors, by repeatedly providing the symbol parenthetically after the object it represents, establish the relationship between the two so well that little conscious effort is required to remember it. If there are significant amounts of intervening text before a symbol is used again, readers may also be pleased to be reminded of its meaning.

However, substituting symbols for words in running text long before they are used in equations can be a significant source of irritation for readers, who must either memorize their definitions or leaf backwards in the paper to remind themselves.

## The Glossary

If enough symbols are used in a paper to warrant inclusion of a glossary, readers can be told of its existence and its location in the paper shortly before any symbols are used. The glossary can be made into a table, say, or put into an appendix, so that it is not a part of the running text and readers feel less compulsion to read it when they encounter it.

Despite the existence of the glossary, however, each new symbol should still be defined when it is first used. The glossary is intended only to remind readers of the definition of a symbol so that they need not search for the place where that particular symbol was first defined and to enable them to understand an equation if they refer to the paper at a later time.

## Conventional Symbol Usage

Many symbols have acquired specific meanings in particular disciplines. For example, the Greek letter rho means "mass density" in fluid mechanics. If an author were to use a different symbol for this parameter, the mathematics would be correct but readers might be needlessly confused. However, it is often useful to briefly define such standard symbols for the benefit of new people entering the field, because of the frequent need for communication across discipline boundaries, and even to remind the author's peers of their meanings.

## Choosing Symbols

In cases where convention does not dictate their choice, letter symbols should be selected that have some relationship to the objects or activities they represent. For example, it would be more reasonable to use the letter $d$ for distance than the letter $t$ or even the letter $x$. Also, the use of single-character symbols creates less confusion in mathematical expressions than the use of multiple-character symbols, and avoiding the letters "l" and "O" eliminates the possibility of confusing them with "one" and "zero."

Computer scientists and programmers, accustomed to assigning meanings somewhat arbitrarily to words in programs, tend not to be as concerned as are other authors about the needs of human readers. For example, if the word *loss* were used in a computer program as a label for the variable *profit*, execution of the program would be unaffected. Authors sometimes use the fact that they have defined their terms as a defense for poor choices. However, even if such authors do define words their way, if their way is not the expected way, readers are likely to be confused if they have already attached other meanings to the same words.

Before leaving the subject of symbols, we note that it is easy for authors to use inadvertently the same symbol to mean different things at different places in the same paper. Also, assigning meanings to symbols and defining abbreviations that are never used in mathematical expressions can impose a needless burden on readers. The goal should be to avoid requiring readers to learn more than a very few new abbreviations in a single paper. Moreover, learning them should clearly benefit the reader, not just the author.

## Jargon and Other Almost Meaningless Words

The irritation that some readers feel when they encounter language understood only in small subcultures results from more than a concern about the corruption of the language. The use of jargon and other undefined terminology in theoretical passages can deny needed information to readers and can prevent them from completing their reading of the paper. Some aspiring authors think that "knowing the terminology" impresses readers, but flaunting such knowledge can be a needless obstacle to communication. Thus, on the one hand, there is seldom justification for using needlessly specialized terminology, which needlessly limits readership, when more widely understood words will do as well. On the other hand, avoiding language commonly used in a particular discipline can result in stilted and wordy substitute phrasing. Authors must find the right language for the expected readers of their particular paper, remembering that their audience includes readers who may be highly qualified but unfamiliar with the language used in the author's immediate environment.

Inexperienced authors should also realize that a term misused within a development team over an extended period comes to sound correct to members of the team. However, it may not to many readers of papers arising from the work of the team.

A related obstacle to understanding is the use of impressive sounding but vacuous words and phrases so cherished by some authors in journals related to, for example, psychology, sociology, and education. Examples include "an interview of client contact," "each progressive step of service-providing," and "the worried-concerned technique"—all of which we have seen recently. The importance of the contributions of these often admirable people may be diminished in the minds of some readers by this pretentiousness.

## WRITING FORMAL AND NOT SO FORMAL MATERIAL

Most of our discussion so far has been aimed at associating real-world meanings with symbols and at relating symbols to each other, based on understood conditions, in order to form abstract models. Manipulation of these logical constructs may be quite formal and mathematical, or it may only involve a carefully written description of the author's chain of reasoning.

Despite the formidable appearance to some readers of more mathematical passages, in some respects they are easier to write. This is partly because the direction taken in the development is largely controlled by the universally agreed upon rules governing mathematical and logical manipulation. In a sense, the author's freedom to make mistakes is limited. Also, the ambiguity so characteristic of the languages used for communication among human beings (as opposed to those for communicating with computers, for example) is greatly reduced.[25] Finally, quite complex relationships among ideas can be expressed in mathematics with remarkable succinctness.

But, as indicated, theoretical material in journal papers cannot always be represented mathematically. Depending on the maturity of the discipline and on the particular work, understanding may be too limited to allow more than a carefully written verbal description of the author's logic.

### Writing Style for Less Formal Logic

Greater precision can usually be achieved in less formal theoretical material if the author uses terse, declarative sentences, with as few subordinate clauses and phrases as possible and with great care exercised in the use of adjectives and adverbs. (Of course, complex sentences should not be shunned to the extent that the author is unable to communicate necessary qualifications and relationships, as seems to be implied by some simplistic measures of "readability.") Information not essential to the logical structure or its manipulation should usually be excluded, since it is likely to be distracting for the reader. For example, consideration of questions about implementation should not be allowed to interfere with the singleness of purpose that should characterize logical developments. Important but supplementary information can be provided later, after the reader has experienced the personal conviction, and pleasure, that some rather complex reasoning does indeed make sense.

### Making Ideas Concrete

Although including currently irrelevant information in theoretical passages can be a source of confusion, it is often useful to remind readers of the relationship between abstract concepts and reality. If use of the running example mentioned earlier is not practicable, a judicious sprinkling of "for examples" throughout theoretical passages can also be effective in establishing concreteness. This device can be helpful to highly intelligent readers who nonetheless have trouble coping with abstractions.

### Confronting the Reader with Puzzles

Computer scientists, mathematicians, and electrical engineers are sometimes obliged to describe "algorithms" in journal papers. These formal procedures are sometimes intended to be implemented in computer programs. They have many of the attributes of other logical developments, and a terse, mathematical or near-mathematical style is appropriate for describing them. However, algorithms, like other logical developments, are sometimes presented without sufficient explanation to allow readers to understand how their purposes are achieved. Instead, the author simply lists in a mechanistic way a sequence of steps. Readers may be obliged in effect to solve a puzzle in order to be convinced that the algorithm works. If such puzzles do not have obvious solutions, readers should be told why the steps in the algorithm are being performed and how their execution accomplishes its purpose.

Some authors of mathematical papers consciously leave uncompleted developments as exercises for their readers. This may be desirable in text books, but many journal readers are too busy to play games, especially ones not planned by the author.

### Level of Detail and Evenness of Presentation

Until now, we have discussed the provision of theoretical material in absolute terms. A step in a logical development is there or it is not; a fact is so or it is not. However, there are gray areas in the writing of theoretical material also. For example, authors must decide how much to expect of their readers. If one part of the theory requires advanced knowledge of some sort, such as higher level mathematics, it makes little sense to include more elementary explanations at another point, such as descriptions of basic set theoretic concepts. If referees and editors fail to intercede, it seems likely that authors of such uneven material will lose one segment of their audience and bore another. This is another of the many cases in which journal authors can help their cause by a shrewd assessment of their audience and by resisting the desire to include needless information simply because they know it themselves.

### When Enough Is Enough

A related determination that authors must make is when to break off mathematical and logical developments, under the assumption that readers can carry on for themselves. A colleague of ours has sometimes expressed exasperation with authors who take too much for granted with the phrase "it is obvious that . . . ," which should never be used unless it is, in fact, obvious. On the other hand, it is tiresome and perhaps a little insulting to some readers to be taken by the hand through obvious developments. The major factor that must be weighted in determining the break-off point is the makeup of the expected audience; if most people in the discipline do not require further development, it should not be provided. Another factor is that the amount of demonstration ought to be related to the expectedness of the result. Less anticipated and less straightforward developments should be spelled out more completely than more obvious and more direct ones. But in seeking the best compromise, we again favor taking a slight risk of boring a few readers, since those readers who are not able to continue are no longer legitimate readers of the paper, not just bored readers. Of course, a terse writing style, in which the more obvious ideas are disposed of quickly, reduces the burden for bright journal readers.

## Overcoming Mind Set

The directions taken in attacking many problems have become conventional, which can put the most creative authors at a disadvantage. The immediate reaction of readers to an unconventional approach taken without warning may be that the author is wrong. Alerting readers beforehand of the new direction can reduce the likelihood of such misunderstandings. One author, whose work we have watched over an extended period, has often encountered negative referee reaction, partly for this reason. It has often taken several years after publication before the real worth of his discoveries has been recognized. Such authors should not just describe their reasoning, but should contrast it with present approaches.

## Putting Aside Other Digressive Material

In the theoretical portions of journal papers, a complete logical justification of the author's results may require derivations, proofs, and explanations that, if included in the running text, would be digressive. For example, a theorem might have to be stated to enable the reader to follow the author's logical strategy, but including its proof at the point where it is stated might interrupt the development. Such material can be placed in appendixes, charts, and tables, for example, to remove it from the main flow. Unfortunately, some readers cannot resist looking at such exhibits as soon as they are referred to, which thwarts the purpose of removing them from the exposition in the first place. There do not appear to be convenient mechanisms for preventing the interruption caused by references to such peripheral material, but placing it near where it is referred to does reduce the impact of the interruption. For example, a nearby table can be found more quickly than an appendix at the back of the paper.

## APPLYING THE THEORY

In many cases, the author of theoretical material in journal papers hopes to convince readers that the new results are also practical. For example, a computer engineer might develop the theoretical basis for computer hardware capable of sorting records at extremely high speed. If this author wants the ideas to be accepted in practice, the paper must not only demonstrate the reasonableness of the scheme in principle but show also, if there is any doubt, that actual hardware configurations can be devised to carry out the sorting.

When logical arguments are used to demonstrate the practicality of theory, authors can expect to encounter more than usual skepticism. Readers will, of course, think that the more formal and mathematical the author's arguments are, the more reliable they are. But readers will also be concerned about factors other than the logicality of the implementation, such as whether its cost is prohibitive or whether development may require further invention. Thus, the author faces a significant challenge in convincing serious readers, who might be considering large investments of development funds. Obviously, any available empirical evidence should be used to abet the author's arguments, but authors should remember too that ill-considered promotional efforts may generate insurmountable sales resistance.

## SAMPLING READER REACTION

It is almost impossible for an author to write a lengthy theoretical passage, especially a less formal one, that can be followed completely by readers. Of course, experienced authors rework their material many times in their attempts to reach this goal. The problem is that the ideas and facts are so familiar to the author that he or she simply fails to anticipate completely the difficulties of readers. And because the author is human, he or she may even have made some errors. The best assurance that an author can get that theoretical arguments have been successfully communicated is the experimental evidence that colleagues have, in fact, been able to follow them.

For the sake of both the author and the reader, reader sampling should be deferred until the author has corrected all problems of which he or she is aware. Ideally, test readers should be chosen who are not familiar enough with the work to be in possession of needed specialized factual information. Moreover, they must be willing workers who will put forth the effort required to read the paper with care. We even suggest that the author not shy away from severe (but not destructive) critics. It is infinitely more desirable that flaws in the paper be detected before its publication than after.

And authors will feel considerably reassured if no serious errors are discovered.

### Taking Criticism Seriously

Authors who have never conducted such tests of their writing skill may be surprised at how their "lucidly" written theoretical passages have been interpreted. However, if ideas are being misunderstood, explanations to reviewers are meaningless; the paper itself must be modified. Also, the author should understand that, even though sentences are completely correct, they may contain near-ambiguities that can confuse readers. And even if the author is able to point out statements in the paper that were overlooked by its reviewers, it is probable that the statements were not presented with sufficient emphasis in the first place.

For any concern whatever expressed by a reviewer, even if it has not been expressed well, the author should assume that something has bothered the reader, should try to determine just what it is, and should then correct it. The author is fortunate to find good reviewers and should take full advantage of their generosity. Conversely, rationalizing criticism can be self-defeating.

## A REASON FOR REJECTION

Although we usually concern ourselves with writing problems in this book, there is one reason for rejecting predominantly theoretical papers that is sufficiently common to justify its mention here. (We note two more reasons for rejection in the next chapter, on writing experimental material.)

### The Paper Tiger

Some theoreticians have a tendency to place too much faith in logic alone. Aristotle, for example, made incorrect statements about the physical characteristics of insects that could have been avoided by simple observation. It is not unusual today to encounter papers, in computer science and electrical engineering, for example, that describe elaborate but not completely formal logical systems, but that provide no experimental evidence that they are workable. If challenged by referees, authors of such papers are apt to defend them with even more "logic." But wary referees generally recognize the difficulties that might be encountered in implementing such ideas, and authors should not be surprised if such papers are rejected.

## SUMMARY

In this chapter we claimed that the successful provision of theoretical information requires an organization no more complicated than need be, but top-down structure was suggested for complex material. Authors were reminded, however, that factors other than organization had to be considered in communicating theoretical information. Currently irrelevant information, for example, was seen as a significant and needless source of confusion.

As many as five kinds of information might be required in theoretical material, although the order in which they might occur in a particular paper was felt to be content-dependent. Comprehension was believed to be enhanced if the audience is informed beforehand of what exactly is to be proved and is kept informed of the strategy throughout. Authors were also reminded of their obligation to relate theoretical constructs to reality when their assumptions are not generally accepted in their discipline. A related requirement was the provision of all facts essential to understanding, such as the significance of mathematical symbols, abbreviations, and "building-block" concepts; authors were also cautioned about taking too much for granted regarding readers' knowledge of jargon and colloquial nomenclature.

Mathematical manipulation was seen as presenting the author with fewer problems than less formal logical developments. Thus, a terse, near-mathematical style was suggested for communicating the latter kind of information, in contrast to the style we advocated for more easily understood material, such as that often appearing in introductions.

The advancement of logical arguments to persuade readers that theory is applicable in practice despite insufficient experimental evidence was seen as being an especially challenging problem for the author, who was advised nonetheless to carefully avoid the "hard sell."

Once authors had a clean draft of their theoretical material, they were advised to test it using colleagues as sample readers. They were encouraged to view all comments objectively and to channel their reactions into modifications of the paper, rather than into debates with reviewers.

The chapter concluded with a brief discussion of a common reason for rejection: claims of new results based on informal logic alone, with inadequate substantiation by experimentation.

The writer of theoretical material might thus begin by describing a self-contained system of notation or comparable prerequisite information, if it were needed. Otherwise, the author might start with a verbal outline of the structure of the passage, possibly with some justification of its organization. Then, a clear explanation of what was to be demonstrated would be given. Assumptions and their rationale would be provided as needed, especially if they were not generally accepted by the author's peers. As the logical or mathematical developments themselves were presented, the author would supply, as it was needed, any factual information necessary to understanding, such as mathematical notation. However, the provision of information not currently needed would be postponed to avoid confusing readers. Throughout the presentation, the author would, as often as seemed appropriate, remind readers on both an organizational basis and in terms of content exactly what was being done.

In our experience, the most common weaknesses in theoretical material are failure to provide all facts needed for understanding, failure to keep readers informed of what is being shown, and failure to establish an appropriate hierarchical organization for complex material. Appendix B is a checklist for authors of theoretical material.

# 4

# *Experimental Material*

The awesome scientific advances of the last few centuries have resulted as much from an appreciation of the need for experimentation as from developing human intellectual capabilities. The scientific method itself is based on this awareness. It is not surprising then that experimental results are usually a key element in journal papers. Indeed, the majority of scientific papers are experimental papers. Moreover, most engineering papers can be characterized as experimental papers.

The remarkable achievements in science and technology generally in recent decades include dramatic progress in statistics, instrumentation, and computational science. These advances have been especially helpful for the experimentalist. Despite this progress, however, the proclivities of human beings for deceiving themselves have not disappeared, and they may reveal themselves in either the investigatory work of the researcher or its presentation in the journal paper. Because of the intimate relationship between the work and its description in the paper, it is not always easy to determine whether weaknesses in the paper are attributable to the methodology of the author or only to the descriptions of it in the paper. Our intention here is to reduce the likelihood that the paper is at fault.

Experimental papers provide facts (often in quantitative form), either with claims that the facts extend theoretical understanding or because they are believed to have intrinsic or practical value. Many experimental papers are straightforward documents in which the author simply provides the facts along with those kinds of information needed for readers to assure themselves of the validity of measured or computed data, to examine the processes used to extract information from the data, and to duplicate the results. In many cases, however, the author of an experimental paper faces significant problems in convincing readers that the data do in fact reflect the phenomena as claimed and that the interpretations of the data are justified.

In this chapter, we discuss six kinds of information that may be required for journal readers to understand and evaluate new experimental results: (1) statements of the purposes of the experiments; (2) explanations of how their designs fulfill their purposes; (3) descriptions of experimental configurations and procedures; (4) presentations of experimental data; (5) observations, conclusions, and opinions arising from the experimental results; and (6) discussions of the broader implications of the experimental findings for the author's discipline. We conclude by identifying two common reasons for the rejection of experimental papers. Appendix C at the end of the book is a checklist that may be useful in helping authors to gage their success in writing the experimental portions of their papers.

In classifying required information, we have taken a finer cut than that of the widely used organization for experimental papers in which an introduction is followed by sections on materials and methods, results, and discussion.[10] Our purpose is to identify needed information more specifically and even to suggest, in a general way, the order in which that information ought to be provided. The standard headings typically used in experimental papers do not specifically identify all needed information. For example, they are not explicit enough about the author's need to justify the design of the experiments or to explain the interpretation of the results.

Unfortunately, we are not quite able to recommend a universal organization for all experimental papers. For example, in a particular case it might not be convenient for an author to justify experimental designs in a separate section and at a particular place in the paper. Instead, that information might have to be woven into a longer passage in which other categories of information are provided. Nonetheless, we do think that our order is suggestive generally. For example, readers ought to understand the purpose of an experiment before they are given details about physical configurations or experimental procedures.

In practice, of course, the kinds of information that we have identified can be included under those subtitles typically used in journals associated with particular disciplines. Realistically, the selection of section headings must take into account the practices followed in the journal for which the paper is intended. However, our categories should help to ensure that all legitimate needs of readers for information are satisfied.

Before discussing our categories of information, we remind readers that many things that were said in the last chapter about writing theoretical passages apply in principle to experimental material as well. We emphasize especially the need for maintaining reader orientation.

## INDICATING THE PURPOSES OF EXPERIMENTS

As the first step in sharing results with professional colleagues, the author of an experimental paper must tell readers what specific purposes the experiments are intended to serve. He or she may also have to restate the purposes and refine the statements of them from time to time throughout the passage to keep readers oriented.

## Supporting Claimed Theoretical Advances

One general purpose that the experiments described in journal papers serve is to provide data to support claims of new theoretical knowledge. Such data are usually obtained from experiments that were designed to confirm hypotheses. But whether the data were obtained by design or accidentally, the author should begin the body by explaining specifically what will be demonstrated with the experiments. If a sequence of experiments is reported, in which the results of one experiment lead to another, several such explanations may be required. This information establishes the context into which all of the details about experimental arrangements and procedures will later be fitted. Conversely, if this information is withheld until a later discussion section (as it sometimes is), the reader will not be equipped to make judgments about the suitability of the experiments as he or she is reading about them. Indeed, the reader may have to return from later parts of the paper to earlier ones to be assured of their appropriateness.

## Providing Useful Data

Experiments conducted to obtain useful data are also described in journal papers, with no claims made about extending theory. In some areas of investigation—behavioral science and sociology, for example—there may be little theoretical structure into which inherently interesting data can be fitted. Also, experimental data often have practical value—to engineers, for example—even though no theoretical advances are based on it. Thus, the experiments described in some journal papers may provide data to be used in making decisions related to the distribution of limited resources to badly needed social programs or to the design of artificial hearts or of high speed trains. If readers are told what purposes such experiments are intended to serve, they can then judge whether the methodology described can indeed provide data that are both pertinent and valid. Of course, this does not rule out the possibility that some readers will use the data in ways not foreseen by the author or even that the data will ultimately lead to improved theoretical understanding.

## Reporting Negative Results

Authors of experimental papers must sometimes take into account the fact that not all experiments produce directly useful information. Negative experimental results may be ignored by the author, may be briefly noted in a paper reporting useful results, or may be described in a separate paper.

Lengthy reports of an unsuccessful experimental effort can easily create impatience in busy journal readers and should usually be omitted from a paper that provides positive results. To do otherwise is just as objectionable as taking readers down blind alleys in theoretical passages. However, by briefly noting some negative results, an author can occasionally save time for fellow investigators who might otherwise waste it duplicating the fruitless experiments. But even here, the amount of space devoted to such material should be limited. Moreover, readers should understand from the outset that no useful results were obtained.

Negative results might also justify publication of a separate paper. For example, if many other researchers are likely to waste significant amounts of time repeating lengthy, costly, but useless experiments, publication of such a paper could preclude needless duplication of effort. In such cases, the separate paper has the advantage of providing readers with enough information so that they can see for themselves that the investigation was carried out properly and thus that the experimentation was indeed unproductive.

## JUSTIFYING EXPERIMENTAL DESIGNS

After readers have been made aware of the purposes of the author's experiments, they must then be convinced that the experiments have been designed such that they are capable of providing the data that they were intended to. The rationale may be so obvious that it need only be mentioned, or it may involve complex and subtle reasoning. Depending on the needs of the particular situation (as suggested previously), this justification may be provided separately or it may pervade the descriptions of the purpose of the experiments and the apparatus and procedures used in carrying them out. Without this justification, however, a mechanistic description of equipment and procedures may fail completely to convince readers that the author's data are actually a measure of anything. To assist inexperienced authors in appreciating this problem, we now examine some of the uncertainties that journal readers may encounter in their attempts to determine whether and to what extent experimental data actually reflect phenomena of interest.

### Uncertainty in Experimental Data

Experimental results may be provided in journal papers in either qualitative or quantitative form. Examples of the former include photographs showing corrosion, wear, or the presence of bacteria, or reported sightings in the Florida Everglades of birds that were thought to be extinct. Such information may have immense scientific importance, but its presentation in a journal paper does not usually confront the author with many problems. After readers have been told what the author is attempting to demonstrate with the observations, they will usually accept them with little question. Of course, as the observations become more unexpected, more convincing evidence will be needed to enhance credibility. And if the author is using such qualitative information to support a hypothesis, he or she will also be obliged to justify the interpretations of the observations.

The goal of much research, however, is to acquire quantitative data. And in the real world of research and development, there are varying degrees of uncertainty in how well the quantitative data provided in journal papers reflect actual phenomena.

*Sources of Uncertainty*

Readers of journal papers are likely to feel considerable faith in numbers acquired from counting. However, a little less confidence can be placed in data gotten from measurements, where, for example, limited precision of instruments and human errors in making and recording measurements can affect results.

Some measurements are extremely difficult, time consuming, and costly to make. Thus, real-world constraints may have prevented the author from taking a sufficient number of measurements to reduce sampling errors. Indeed, it may only be the remarkable ingenuity of the author that has enabled him or her to gather any data at all.

Hardware prototypes and mock-ups, usually simplified and constructed on a different scale from the equipment they are intended to imitate, are often used to gather experimental data when time, cost, or other constraints prevent measurement of actual phenomena or when equipment being designed does not yet exist. An example is data acquired from tank testing models of boat hulls. Uncertainty may exist in such data because the essential features of the imitated activity may not have been completely captured in the prototype. For example, errors of scale may have influenced results.

Abstract models may themselves be the subjects of journal papers, as was assumed to be the case with the econometric model used as an example in the last chapter. But mathematical models are also used extensively to generate data, with quantities that cannot be measured directly calculated from those that can. Data obtained from simple established relationships—Ohm's law, for example—can be quite reliable, and numerical information resulting from their application usually presents few problems for journal readers. In properly designed experiments, modeling errors can even be estimated statistically.

However, as more approximations are introduced into mathematical models, readers cannot have as much confidence in the results. The numerical methods used to solve equations on digital computers may introduce even more uncertainty. Data produced by computer simulation and by probabilistic modeling become increasingly less reliable as the model becomes a more simplified representation of the modeled activity. Yet, these are increasingly important sources of the data that appear in journal papers.

If a mathematical model of a complex system is, in fact, an amalgam of smaller models, with less formal relationships established among the elements, the likelihood that the configuration will produce meaningful data is even further reduced. Such tandem modeling systems might be used in the computer industry, for example, to model semiconductor manufacturing processes, device physics, and circuit behavior, with important and costly decisions based on the results they provide.

Examination of submitted manuscripts reveals another problem: Some authors have limited knowledge of statistics. One evidence of this fact is that quantitative data may be presented with insufficient information to enable readers to estimate how much confidence to put in them. Because experimentation is often costly and time consuming, statisticians have given considerable attention to the design of experiments that can produce greater amounts of reliable information from lesser amounts of experimental effort. (Some sophisticated experimental designs including practical examples related to computer performance are described by Schatzoff.[26]) Also, a great deal of attention has been given by statisticians to separating the effects of experimental factors. However, authors trained in other disciplines are not usually knowledgeable about such sophisticated applications of statistics. (Psychologists seem to be a notable exception.)

*Implications for the Author*

Because of these uncertainties, authors of journal papers have an obligation that permeates the writing of all experimental material: Supply readers with as much relevant information as possible to enable them to determine for themselves how much confidence to put in the data provided. Readers must be able to repeat the author's experiments with the expectation of getting the same results that he or she did.

For example, experiments may have been conducted to demonstrate the feasibility of or to predict the performance of equipment that has not yet been built. It is not enough to describe what measurements or calculations were made and how they were made; it is also necessary for the author to explain the reasoning used to conclude that the data do indeed reflect the phenomena attributed to them.

If the methodology used allows statistically significant amounts of data to be acquired and if the author's training permits him or her to reduce the data in ways that are statistically acceptable, of course, that should be done. This may well reveal intelligence in the data that would not otherwise be evident. However, the author of a journal paper should carefully avoid engaging in unintentional statistical sleight-of-hand. If knowledgeable readers see statistical flaws in a journal paper, they are likely to reject out of hand all of the author's results, even though the basic data are actually valid. Instead, the author should describe in a straightforward way how the data were obtained and why the meaning attributed to them is justified.

If it is physically possible to obtain statistically meaningful amounts of data, but the author is not competent to process it, he can also use a statistician as a coauthor of the paper or as a consultant. An obvious long-term solution is to equip himself or herself better to cope with the statistical aspects of research. Basic texts on statistics describe how to make measurements and to reduce and display results so that readers can better assess them (see the Notes at the end of the book[27-29]); another useful basic book on conducting experiments and presenting experimental results is that by Baird.[30]

## DESCRIBING CONFIGURATIONS AND PROCEDURES

The equipment and procedures involved in conducting some experiments can be so elaborate that several manuals would be required to describe them completely. Nonetheless, journal readers must understand the conditions under which the data were gathered. The objective then is to seek ways to reduce the amount of space devoted to their description without denying the reader essential information. For example, the use of illustrations to supplement text can often result in more efficient use of space than the use of words alone. Standard, commercially available equipment need only be identified, not described, since its characteristics are either known or can easily be obtained by readers. (Inexperienced authors often think that such descriptions would be a convenience for readers, but efficiency would be reduced if the same equipment were described in many papers.) And, in disciplines where standard test procedures are used, they need not be described to the author's peers; only the procedure itself need be identified.

### Relevant Factors in Experimental Configuration

The amount of attention given to nonstandard components in experimental configurations ought to be related to the amount of influence they can be expected to have on results. There is usually little point, for example, in devoting space to the description of a clamp used routinely to hold another piece of equipment. Such details should be included only when it is known that they have affected results or when it cannot be certain that they have not.

We find that inexperienced authors tend to provide too much rather than too little information. Thus, they leave the task of deciding what is relevant to their readers. The tendency of some authors to provide too much detail may stem from requirements placed on them as students. But the purpose of laboratory reports was to assure the instructor that the student followed prescribed procedures correctly. In the professional world, the author is assumed to have had such training and can omit much of that detail from journal papers.

Prototypes and models, including mathematical models, should also be regarded as experimental configurations. As implied earlier, competent readers can work their way through the mathematics, but they must also understand and be convinced of the reasonableness of the assumptions on which the mathematics is based. In our experience, papers involving statistics and probability cause the most controversy among referees.

We recall a paper that described a probabilistic model. The proof that its predictions corresponded with reality was that they agreed reasonably well with the results of computer simulation of the same activity. However, validating evidence for the simulator had never been published. Although some credibility was lent to the results because somewhat similar data had been obtained from two seemingly independent sources, readers should have been told that the simulator output had not been validated experimentally. Actually, in this case, both the model and the simulator had been produced by the same team of investigators, and both might have been based on similar but incorrect assumptions, with neither reflecting reality.

### Experimental Procedures

In some cases, the quantitative results presented in experimental papers are obtained by straightforward measurements. In many cases, however, considerable ingenuity is required of the author, who must provide enough details to enable readers to duplicate the procedures. However, as was the case with describing experimental configurations, inexperienced authors tend to provide too much unessential information. Even if readers do choose to duplicate the work of an author, they need not be told everything, any more than the plans for building a house need specify where every nail should be driven. Those aspects of the procedure that caused the author the greatest difficulties and that can be expected to have influenced the results should be described with the greatest care.

### PRESENTING EXPERIMENTAL DATA

Despite the importance of the original design of an experiment, the configuration and characteristics of test equipment, and the methodology used, in the final analysis it is the numbers that count. This all important quantitative data may be presented in journal papers in any or all of several forms.

So far we have made a clear distinction between data believed to have intrinsic or practical value and those used to extend theoretical understanding. In practice, this distinction may not be quite so clear cut. Measurements that have never been made before may have immediate practical value, for example, in the manufacture of magnetic recording tape. The same measurements may also be interesting for their own sake in the sense that they provide insight into the phenomena measured, even if that insight is insufficient to extend theory. And the same data might ultimately become a stepping stone to greater theoretical understanding. The amount of data presented and the form in which it is presented should be based on what the author plans to do with it in the paper and how the reader is expected to use it.

First, data should never be provided in journal papers without an explicitly stated purpose. It is unreasonable to expect busy editors, referees, and readers to attempt to see value in data when even the author has failed to do so. In determining the suitability of papers for publication, referees assess whether the author's claims of value for experimental results (made primarily in the introduction) are justified. If the author makes no such claims, referees are given no reason for recommending publication.

Data provided in support of a hypothesis may be presented in a variety of forms and quantities, as needed to demonstrate the thesis of the author. But data not relevant for this purpose, even if they might have other value for some readers, should be omitted. Data that are not pertinent to the author's aims can easily lead to reader confusion.

Data that are believed to have intrinsic or practical value, on the other hand, should be provided generously. The justification for providing the data is that the mathematics, the equipment, the knowledge, or the time needed for users of the data to generate more of their own is presumably lacking. And, of course, the data should be presented in forms that can be expected to be most convenient for their anticipated uses.

**The Need for Raw Data**

An author should generally attempt to supply some raw data, that is, data presented so that individual values can be seen. All too often, authors of submitted manuscripts provide graphs plotted from experimental data in which individual data points are obscured. Or the data are reduced or normalized in ways that hide individual values. Readers may be given no idea of how many measurements were actually made or of how much variation existed among the individual measurements. Yet, the readers of some papers are expected to use the quantitative information directly. And those readers who choose to duplicate the work of the author should be provided with samples of data to make realistic comparisons with their own results. Many readers also carefully examine the data provided in journal papers, and they may even discover meaning in them that was overlooked by the author.

**Summarized Data**

Despite the usefulness of raw data, sometimes the amount of data amassed by a researcher is too voluminous to be presented in other than summary form. In such instances, the author should describe the data collecting and summarizing process in sufficient detail so that the reader can make judgments about its validity. Even in this case, however, samples of raw data are desirable for the reasons previously mentioned.

## Excessive Amounts of Data

Statisticians are continually extending our understanding of the significance of computed and measured results, including those obtained from probabilistic models and from computer simulation. Of course, the procedures used in acquiring such results should be reported in such a way that readers can see the extent of their validity. However, because of the uncertainties discussed earlier, it is not always possible to estimate precisely how well experimental data reflect phenomena of interest because of the indirect means researchers often must resort to in acquiring them. But when there is considerable uncertainty about the meaningfulness of data, providing great volumes of data may not be convincing either. Computers have made the generation of data so easy that some authors attempt to overwhelm readers with sheer quantity. In a well-designed experiment, general conclusions inferred from a small sample may have a much higher confidence level than conclusions drawn from a very large sample in a poorly designed experiment. When considerable uncertainty exists, additional evidence may have to be provided instead from separately designed experiments in order for referees and other readers to accept the results.

Conversely, some inexperienced authors submit manuscripts in which too little or no data are provided. The reader of a journal paper should never be asked to accept interpretations of experimental results based on such statements as "the data we acquired demonstrate to our satisfaction that . . . ." Failure to provide actual data in a journal paper conflicts with the requirement of journal publication that readers be able to determine for themselves whether the author's claims are correct. The popular phrase "studies have shown" has no place in journal papers.

## Getting Around Publication Restrictions

Scientists and engineers are not always free to publish experimental data, because of proprietary and national security considerations. A common way that this constraint is circumvented (with the approval of the appropriate authorities, of course) is to present only relative data and to show trends without showing absolute values. The more information that can be provided, of course, the better. For example, if the author is allowed to indicate whether scales are linear or logarithmic, the reader is given a little more insight. But these kinds of restrictions seriously complicate matters for other researchers who attempt to duplicate the author's results, and they greatly limit the value of the paper to readers who might want to use the data directly. Nonetheless, in some cases, referees may conclude that enough can be learned from such a paper by the author's peers to justify its publication. However, many journals automatically reject such censored submissions.

## Making Data Meaningful

Experimental results would usually be incomprehensible if each measured value were only presented in isolation. Thus, it is the author's obligation to present data in ways that allow readers to see the trends and patterns and to make the comparisons that the author did in extracting information from the data. The variety of ways that authors can use to reduce and present data so as to reveal the intelligence contained in them is almost limitless. Considerable attention has been given to the handling of data and the preparation of graphs and tables. We again suggest that readers examine basic texts on statistics[27-29] and the previously mentioned book on experimentation.[30] Some useful suggestions for the preparation of tables are also provided by Arnold.[31]

## Facilitating the Making of Comparisons

We add here a few additional and possibly obvious comments about graphs that might make journal papers more helpful to readers. Of course, scales should be chosen that reveal the greatest amount of relevant information. But on occasion it might be important for readers to compare the author's results with previously reported data, which can be facilitated if the author uses the same scale as was used in the cited paper.

The author will obviously present data so that comparisons can easily be made within his or her own paper. Whether particular graphs to be compared are placed beside each other or one on top of the other often affects how easily their differences and similarities can be seen. Although the author cannot always control the placement of figures, graphs that are to be compared can sometimes be combined in a single composite figure, with the relative placement of the elements being of the author's own choosing.

## Computer Output

The ability to generate data by computer can be immensely helpful to researchers, but it can also create problems for journal readers. Unedited computer listings sometimes contain extraneous letters and numbers that are meaningless to the uninitiated. Moreover, both the structure and legibility of computer printouts can be almost incomprehensible. The quality of the output of newer computer printers is vastly improved over their predecessors, but still there is never any justification to penalize readers so as to provide the author with the convenience of computer generated data, figures, or text. For example, if exponents cannot be generated as superscripts, the alternative should be conventional mathematical notation that is familiar to the majority of readers, not one peculiar to a particular programming language. Despite their shortcomings, some of the remarkable graphics capabilities provided by computers can also enhance the presentation of experimental data, as demonstrated by Tufte.[32]

**Providing Experimental Conditions with the Data**

A mundane but practical problem associated with exhibits of experimental data is where to provide the conditions under which they were obtained: in the text, in the caption, or on the figure itself. A basic principle in writing journal papers is to provide information only once, both to save time for readers and to avoid the confusion that might result if readers believed that the duplicated information was actually something new. This principle should be carried through as far as possible in the presentation of experimental data.

The goal of efficiency in journal papers is not furthered by repeating information in text, figures, and tables. Any duplication should be justified on the basis of significant benefits to readers. It is especially irritating to read a lengthy passage, find a reference to a figure at the end, and then discover that the information could be seen at a glance in the figure. The best medium for communicating each particular kind of information should be sought.

If substantial amounts of information are required for a reader to understand the significance of an exhibit, that information should probably be provided in the text, especially if comparisons are to be made with other exhibits. On the other hand, if exhibits are expected to be used primarily for reference purposes and if the information is not too lengthy, the figures may be made into self-contained entities, with most of the conditions provided either on the figures themselves or in their captions.

There is at least one good reason for incorporating as much information as possible into the caption, rather than on the figure. Because of limited space on figures, authors sometimes resort to the use of confusing abbreviations and legends that can present an avoidable hurdle for readers.

Lengthy footnotes to tables (which are typically set in smaller size type) can also be a source of frustration to readers. If these readers must frequently transfer their attention from table entries to footnotes, especially if the footnotes are unduly long, it might be preferable to provide the information in the supporting text or in the table caption instead.

**Overly Complex Figures**

Some authors take pride in the great amount of information that they can provide in a single figure or table. However, "busy" figures and complex tables that require excessive time to be deciphered are also inconsistent with the efficiency goal of journal communication.

### Figure Captions

The essence of experimental results are often presented in figures of some sort. Yet, figure captions in submitted experimental papers are often simple, uninformative labels. Indeed, the same caption is sometimes used for several figures, with the reader left to determine differences by examining the figures themselves. An excellent opportunity to make experimental papers more useful is to seriously consider just what information readers need about each figure.

## DERIVING INFORMATION FROM EXPERIMENTAL DATA

It is not unusual to see a submission from an inexperienced author in which careful descriptions of experimental designs and presentations of experimental results are followed by informal discussions that are an unfortunate mixture of observations, opinions, speculation, and conclusions. Just as it was necessary for journal readers to understand how quantitative data were acquired, it is also essential that they understand the mental processes of the author in deriving knowledge from the data.

Experimental data may give rise to three kinds of information: directly observed intelligence, logically inferred conclusions, and informed opinions. Their differences may be more obvious if we consider a simple example.

### Observations Arising from Experimental Data

Examination of data acquired in a study of errors in computer programs might reveal that more errors always occurred in sequences containing certain instructions. Although the author might have to call the attention of his readers to this fact, the information is inherent in the data.

The author might even make deeper observations. For example, it might be noted that the instructions associated with errors were more complex in their effects than most other instructions. For instance, these instructions might cause different actions to be taken depending on the values stored at certain locations in the computer memory. This information too is inherent in the experimental data, and anyone provided with the data and having knowledge of the computer's instruction set would have no quarrel with the author's observation.

No inferences or opinions are involved in deriving any of this information. The author is simply making his readers aware of the facts.

### Inferring Conclusions from Experimental Data

A conclusion might also be inferred from these data, and that is an entirely different matter. Conclusions involve inductive reasoning and always imply prediction. In our case, for example, the author might conclude that the use of more complex instructions in computer programs, even instructions different from those indicated above, would inevitably result in equally high occurrences of errors. This conclusion might be correct, but it also might not be.

In order to legitimately make such a claim, the author of a journal paper would be obliged to provide sufficient experimental evidence to justify this prediction. Actually, instead of the conclusion inferred by the author above, the syntax of the instructions associated with higher error rates might have been so unnatural (a different kind of complexity) that programmers had a greater tendency to make mistakes in coding them. Instructions that were equally complex in terms of their effects, but were at the same time easier to use, might well have a different effect on error rates. Without experimental confirmation of such a hypothesis, an author is not free to claim such a conclusion, although it might be offered as an opinion.

The hazards of inferring universally correct conclusions from a relatively small number of observations are well known to most experienced journal readers. A fortuitous combination of events, especially when combined with an investigator's eagerness to believe that he or she has made a great discovery, can easily be misleading. Awareness of the risks inevitably leads readers to carefully scrutinize the conclusions reported in journal papers, a fact that authors should keep in mind as they write this part of the paper.

We recall an experiment that was described to us in a psychology course. Both hungry and fed rats were placed at the entrance to a maze, and food was placed at the exit. The hungry rats found their way through the maze more quickly than the fed rats, demonstrating, we were told, that hungry rats can think more clearly than fed rats. We were also given some advice based on these experimental results—take tests on an empty stomach.

## Offering Opinions Based on Experimental Results

The third kind of information that may arise directly from experimental data is the author's informed opinions about the results. Although we use the word opinion, such observations and comments may have considerable justification. After having thought about the work for months or even years, the author's depth of understanding can make his or her opinions about the results one of the most useful parts of the paper. Moreover, these insights can provide significant motivation for readers to do additional research, one of the basic purposes of journal publication in the first place.

However, there should be no doubt in the reader's mind that the author is expressing opinions and, moreover, that the author knows it. And even then, the opinions should be plausible to the author's peers. In keeping with the principles of scientific journalism, the author should avoid the appearance of being opinionated by sharing the rationale for his or her views with the reader. Any evidence of dogmatism or bias can quickly lead skeptical journal readers to reject completely all of the author's views. Journal readers are usually too busy to separate the wheat from the chaff.

## Distinguishing among Kinds of Information

Because of the possibility of reader confusion, we favor a clear separation of observations based on experimental data from predictions made from such observations (conclusions), as well as from informed opinions. But even if an author feels that physical separation is not practicable in a particular case, his or her awareness of these differences can reduce the likelihood of their being confused in the paper. The author can make the distinctions instead by the phrasing of individual sentences.

Another distinction can help to avoid reader confusion. As may be gathered from our earlier discussion of the uses of experimental data, formal conclusions may not appear in all journal papers. When they are presented, conclusions in the formal sense should be distinguished from summaries. Summaries serve a different purpose in primary journal papers and are discussed in the next chapter.

## THE IMPLICATIONS OF EXPERIMENTAL RESULTS

Observations, conclusions, and opinions arising from experimental results may have broader implications for the author and the discipline. These implications may be incorporated into the concluding section, as discussed in the next chapter, or they may be of sufficient length to justify a separate discussion section. In the latter case, the concluding section might simply present, with the other kinds of information that we discuss in the next chapter, a summary of the discussion provided here.

The distinction we make between opinions stemming directly from experimental data and the broader implications of the results may be clearer if we return to our example about errors in computer programs. Our growing dependence on computers makes errors in computer programs increasingly important to our entire society. After having done the experiments, our hypothetical author might have thought about computer errors in a more general way over an extended period. He or she might have concluded, for example, that some characteristics of programming languages commonly used by members of a particular profession are inconsistent with the way these users normally think about and express the problems they solve on computers. Although the author would not be justified in inferring this conclusion without experimental evidence, the author's opinion might nonetheless be quite valuable. Appropriate further research might even be suggested, another topic we discuss in the next chapter. Thus, discussing the broader implications of experimental results can extend even further the benefits of research.

Of course, such implications are still only informed opinions, and the admonitions made earlier about expressing opinions still apply. In fact, there is even greater peril here for the inexperienced author. If missionary work is carried out too zealously, skeptical journal readers might begin to question the author's ability to do objective research.

## TWO MORE REASONS FOR REJECTION

In discussing theoretical material in journal papers, we mentioned a common reason for rejection. We add two more here, both related to predominantly experimental papers.

### Unjustified Theoretical Claims

Theoreticians have always had a tendency to explain the world around them by using logic alone. Some prospective journal authors are so hasty in concluding that they have made a great theoretical discovery that they attach unwarranted significance to inherently interesting experimental results. Their paper is then rejected because referees were given insufficient bases for accepting their claims. Had these authors presented the same results without the extravagant claims, their papers might have been accepted and their results made available to their professional colleagues.

### The Exaggerated Result Paper

Papers that claim a result that does not hold up are simply rejected. But a more difficult problem is posed by the paper that claims a broader result than the experimental evidence justifies. If referees and editors detect exaggeration in an author's claims, even if the paper has something to contribute, they may become impatient about finding the exact boundaries of the results. Again, a paper that might have been accepted had the author's claims been expressed more modestly is instead rejected because its reviewers were not able to see the precise limits of the contribution.

## SUMMARY

It was claimed in this chapter that experimental papers provide facts, usually in the form of quantitative data, either to support claims of theoretical advances or because the facts are believed to have intrinsic or practical value. We contended that readers needed as many as six kinds of information from an experimental paper.

Authors were advised to begin by describing their purpose in providing experimental results so as to establish the framework into which all subsequent details would later be fitted. In many cases, the author would also be required to convince readers that the experiments could indeed provide the data needed to achieve their stated purposes. Authors were also reminded of the possible difficulties faced by readers in assessing the validity of experimental data.

Efficiency in describing experimental arrangements and procedures was recommended so that readers would be made aware of possible influences on test results but would at the same time not be encumbered with needless details.

Samples of raw experimental data were believed to be useful to journal readers in a variety of ways, even when the volume of data was such that it had to be presented in summarized form. However, in papers that claimed to advance theoretical knowledge, authors were advised to omit data not relevant for that purpose to avoid confusion, even if the data were believed to have other value. Several publications were identified that might help authors in reducing and presenting experimental data.

Experimental data were said to give rise to three distinct kinds of information, which authors were advised to carefully distinguish, at least in their own minds: intelligence derived directly from observation of the data; conclusions logically inferred from them; and informed opinions by the author about the experimental results.

Experimental results might also have longer term implications for the author and the discipline; these might be presented in a separate discussion section. It was said that such material could result in even greater exploitation of the investment in research and development.

The chapter concluded by noting two frequent reasons for the rejection of experimental papers: the failure to prove hastily made theoretical claims based on experimental results; and the making of exaggerated claims.

In summary, then, the author of experimental material in a journal paper might begin with a description of the purposes of the experiments and with a careful explanation of how their designs enable their purposes to be realized. Standard experimental procedures would simply be identified; nonstandard experimental arrangements and procedures would be described in sufficient detail to reveal possible effects on results and to allow duplication, but pointless details would be omitted in the interests of efficiency. Observations based directly on factual information available to readers would be separated from logically induced conclusions and from the author's opinions about the results. Long-term implications of the author's results to the discipline might justify treatment in a separate section.

In our experience, the most common weaknesses in experimental material are failure to establish beforehand the purposes of the experiments to be described, failure to provide enough information about the data acquired, and poorly reasoned discussions of results. Appendix C may be useful to authors in checking their experimental material.

# 5

# *Openings and Closings*

Efficiency in communicating the results of research is one of the three characteristics that we associated with the primary journal paper in Chapter 1. Since in a truly efficient paper nothing is included that does not serve a purpose, the small number of words in those parts of the paper that have not yet been discussed in detail should not be the sole measure of their importance. In this chapter and the next, we consider the roles of the remaining elements of the journal paper.

Here, we first consider some more desirable repetition, this time involving the title, the abstract, and the introduction. Next, we discuss the purposes and the preparation of the title and the abstract, which jointly select the audience for further reading. These widely circulated elements expose the author's results to a far larger audience than the entire readership of the journal in which the complete paper is published. Finally, we treat closings, which summarize the relationship between the scientific evidence presented in the body and the contribution claimed in the introduction, consider the significance of the new results for the author's discipline, and suggest possible directions for future research. A well prepared closing can help the author to realize the potential of his or her contribution for influencing the work of fellow researchers.

## MORE DESIRABLE REPETITION

The title, the abstract, and the introduction of a primary journal paper have similar purposes and provide similar information to achieve them. The three jointly direct the attention of readers with increasing specificity to the subject of the paper. The title, by providing some information about the subject of the paper, selects from a large prospective audience those readers who might profit from reading the abstract. The abstract, in turn, screens its smaller audience to retain only those readers who ought to go on to the introduction. However, the information in each of these parts is included for its own sake for those who do not read further, in addition to being a means to an end for those who do. If these elements are written well, those who choose not to read further will at least have learned something about the contribution.

In discussing the introduction in Chapter 2, we noted the not-uncommon problem of referees not being able to identify the contribution. Since the functions of the title and the abstract are achieved primarily by providing information about the contribution, they afford the first opportunities to communicate this essential information. Some attention may also be given in titles and abstracts to the implications of the new findings and to how they were obtained. Unlike introductions, however, there is seldom enough space in titles and abstracts to do an adequate job in any of these areas, and often nothing can be done about fitting the new results into the context of present knowledge.

It is clear then that, in performing the attention-focusing and filtering functions, some information provided in the title is repeated in the abstract and again in the introduction. But on each occasion, the information is expanded considerably, with perhaps a tenfold increase in the number of words in going from one level to the next. This journalistic strategy is commonly used in newspapers, with each iteration of the story repeating information included at the previous level but also providing additional details. We think it has considerable merit from a pedagogical point of view, and its use is one more justified exception to the general rule of striving for brevity in journal papers. It is also efficient, despite the repetition, because many prospective readers who would not benefit from further reading are filtered out at each level.

This technique can also be useful in attaining the goal alluded to above. It helps authors to reward their readers with some useful information no matter where in the paper they stop reading. (Of course, this aim cannot usually be achieved in the body, which must often be read entirely for readers to see the validity of the author's claims.)

## THE TITLE

The title of the journal paper may be included with or without the abstract in separately published indexes and in data retrieval systems, it will be listed in the table of contents of the journal in which the paper is published, and it will appear with the published paper itself. Although the abstract shares with the title the duty of screening readers, the even more widely circulated title represents the first exposure of the author's results to the prospective reader. This fact should be taken into account in apportioning time and thought to its preparation.

We first consider the need for complete honesty in the title of a journal paper, where we discuss specifically bad first impressions from the title itself, failure of the paper to live up to the expectations created by the title, and failure of the title to adequately represent the contribution. Then we consider four kinds of information that may be included in the title: the area in which the contribution was made, the contribution and its limits, its significance to the discipline, and how it was achieved. Finally, we comment on appropriate language for the title of a journal paper.

## The Need for Candor

The goal of efficiency in primary journal papers requires complete honesty in the title. In order neither to exclude readers who ought to read the paper nor to waste the time of those who ought not, the title should indicate neither no more nor no less than the paper has to offer. The effectiveness of the title should be measured in terms of how good of a decision it has enabled the prospective reader to make, not how many readers were induced to read more of the paper.

### Bad First Impressions from the Title

The title of a journal paper can influence readers' opinion of the author as well as their decisions about further reading, even if the reading decision is negative. Although most nonreaders will be left with neutral feelings, some may form negative opinions if the title has a promotional tone or includes "buzz" words. For example, "dramatic," "new and improved," "high quality," and "space-age technology" are unsuitable in the titles of journal papers. In a world in which advertising is so pervasive, it is sometimes difficult for the inexperienced author to understand that some kinds of efforts to sell new results may actually dissuade unknown colleagues from further reading. Even after this notion is accepted in principle, continual vigilance is required for the author to remain aware of lapses into salesmanship. Some exceptionally brilliant people, who have earned doctorates at leading universities, are unable to distinguish between scientific and promotional arguments.

Authors can alienate prospective readers in other ways as well, such as by attempting to make their titles witty, clever, or cute. Some readers may have a different sense of humor from that of the author, may have no sense of humor, or more likely think that humor has no place in journal papers.

Journal authors have another less obvious professional obligation in the writing of titles (as well as other parts of journal papers). Headlines in newspapers and magazines are designed to attract readers. In less responsible ones, headlines may be deliberately misleading. Although journal authors are not likely to approach such levels of sensationalism, it must be remembered that journal paper titles may be seen by readers having much less knowledge of the discipline than the author and the author's peers. For example, a newspaper reporter who misunderstood a carelessly worded title might pass on misinformation. If this were done in the case of, say, a medical or pharmaceutical discovery, possibly unfortunate consequences for the public could result.

## Disappointing Those Who Read Further

The more of the paper that is read, the greater is the potential for the title to create negative feelings, because more time can be wasted by disappointed readers. Growing frustration may be felt by the reader who has not been able to determine from an imprecise title or from subsequent reading exactly what the contribution is. If the reader assumes from the title that the author has new results to report, but discovers that little or no original information is actually provided, disappointment is even more likely. But the author who tricks busy colleagues into further reading by overstating the results in the title is likely to cause the most profound resentment.

## Underselling the Results

In contrast to the would-be salesman, a few authors are actually too modest in their titles. In an ideal world, the results of research and development should be made known and available to all who can benefit from them; in reality, of course, commercial and national security considerations often preclude this from happening. But if the author is free to publish the results, he or she has an obligation, in addition to a personal stake, in announcing the contribution as completely and as specifically as space allows.

The title should claim the most general result that is justified by the scientific corroboration included in the paper. For example, if a technique were developed that could be used to schedule city buses, a broad enough title should be sought so as not to exclude its use in scheduling parts flow in an assembly operation, if that were also possible. Or if the author had formulated a synthetic lubricant with good high-temperature characteristics, if it could also be produced cheaply, the author should try to communicate that information as well. Such complete announcements help to ensure that the investment in research will be rewarded by the new results being exploited as widely as possible. And it is obviously in the author's best interest to do so.

Authors of papers that contribute original knowledge should also try to subtly establish that fact in their titles (or at least in their abstracts). Although it might be assumed that the paper would not be published in a primary journal unless it did report new results, it might actually appear in a publication that mixes journal papers with other kinds of articles (some periodicals do). In any case, its title (and abstract) will be included in indexes and information retrieval systems among the titles and abstracts of other kinds of articles. Thus, the author might suggest the originality of the contribution in the title by using words such as "new," "original," and "novel."

## Focusing on the Area of the Contribution

The attention of readers is best focused by the title on the areas of specialization in which new contributions are made by a judicious trade-off between specificity and generality. The area is identified as specifically as possible without unwittingly screening out prospective readers. Broad classifications, such as design automation or marine biology, do little for specialists. Categories that are too narrow, on the other hand, may exclude prospective readers working in closely allied areas (near peers) who might be interested in the new results.

For example, a title might indicate that a new syntax checker, intended for use in a compiler for a particular high-level computer programming language, had been designed. Enough words are included in the previous sentence to identify the subject area for most readers who are even slightly familiar with computer software. In practice, the author would have to pare down the large number of words in this example based on the expected audience. Since only designers of language processors are likely to be interested in a syntax checker, some of the more general terms could be omitted. Readers of this paper would probably want to know only that the design for a new syntax checker was reported and the identity of the language for which it was intended. If the paper were meant for publication in a journal that specialized in computer science, that too would help to indicate the area of the contribution. (The perceived editorial focus of the journal itself screens readers.) However, if the author coined a new term for the algorithm underlying the syntax checker, introducing that term might better be deferred until the introduction. Catchy words and phrases that may ultimately become associated with the author's work are desirable, but they should be withheld until they can be suitably defined.

We were present when such a term was coined. A former editor of the *IBM Systems Journal*, Lyle Johnson, "wasted" several hours trying to find a suitable word for a hidden-to-the-user high-speed memory used in a then-new IBM computer. The resulting term, "cache memory," is now used extensively throughout the computer industry and probably earned some recognition for the authors of the papers in which it was originally used.

## Identifying the Contribution and Establishing Its Limits

The most important information conveyed by the title of a journal paper is that which identifies the contribution. In the example of the syntax checker above, it should be noted that none of our many words identify a contribution. Syntax checkers have been around for a long time, and making another one is not necessarily a contribution. In this case, the new syntax checker might detect errors at an earlier stage in the compilation process, say, or be easily adaptable for use with many different languages.

Readers should not only be given information about the nature of the contribution but should even be given some feeling for its limits. For example, a new antibiotic might be effective against several specific strains of bacteria. A new bilge pump for pleasure vessels might remove water at an 11-percent higher rate with the same amount of human effort. A new valve arrangement for internal combustion engines might improve their efficiency by exactly 3 percent.

The extent of some contributions can be communicated by making quantitative comparisons with the present state of the art. When quantification is not possible, less specific comparisons are better than no comparisons at all. Even "much greater than" suggests something a little different from "greater than," for example, which is itself not very precise. Yet, the mathematical notation exists even for making this distinction, suggesting its usefulness in the most rigorous of disciplines.

## Indicating Significance

If the significance of a new contribution is not obvious to the author's peers, explicitly suggesting it in the title can sometimes motivate further reading without undue risk of disappointing readers.

The most basic measure of significance, as indicated in the discussion of introductions in Chapter 2, is the extent to which fundamental understanding is advanced by the new information. Identifying in the title the contribution and its limits is usually all that can be done to convey this kind of information. Occasionally, however, it might be desirable to suggest the implications of more practical, less specialized discoveries. For example, if a dramatically faster method for finding square roots in digital computers were discovered, readers might not recall how often square roots are taken in scientific computations, and the author might attempt to remind them. Thus, the extent of the contribution would be conveyed by noting the increase in speed, and its significance by suggesting how often that speed advantage was likely to be realized. In this case, the words "frequently encountered" might suggest the importance of the contribution. The significance of other contributions might be their potential for practical application. For example, data gathered about drug use in certain segments of society might have potential for increasing the effectiveness of antidrug campaigns.

If the significance of a contribution seems at all improbable, however, it is better not to suggest it in the title. Too little space is available to even hint at substantiation. Moreover, the reader at this point has too little information about the author to put much faith in claims of significance. Some readers may never read far enough to learn that the author's claims might be justified. Indeed, as the implications of new results become increasingly speculative, a point is reached where they should not be mentioned anywhere in the journal paper. Less experienced authors cannot overestimate how objectionable such projections can be to some seasoned journal readers.

Also, as significance becomes more obvious to the author's peers, he or she should become increasingly reluctant to mention it in the title. Telling colleagues what everybody in the field already knows does more than waste precious space. It can sound patronizing to intelligent journal readers.

More popular measures of significance than those used by the author's peers should also be avoided in titles. To do otherwise can sound like an appeal to less discerning readers.

## Suggesting Methodology

The strategy used in deriving the new information or achieving the new result reported in a journal paper should be suggested in the title if it was unusual and likely to be of interest to prospective readers. For example, one more experimental paper in some particular area of sociology might not be of interest, but an original explanation of many previous observations might be welcome. In this case, a form of the word "theory" might be appropriate. Adjectives such as "analytical," "statistical," and "experimental" can also suggest approaches. Identifying standard experimental procedures in areas of biology and physiology, for example, can provide information about the way that new results were obtained.

New methodology sometimes leads to new discoveries, in which case a paper might actually represent dual contributions. For example, a new modeling technique might have permitted the author to better explain behavior of memory hierarchies in computers. The approach might also have the potential for modeling city traffic patterns or other phenomena. In this case, an attempt should be made to reflect in the title both the discovery of a new modeling technique, as well as its fruitful application.

Of course, if the methodology were actually the contribution, the emphasis in the title would automatically reflect that fact, since the primary objective of the title is to identify the contribution.

## Using the Language of the Author's Peers

Each word in the title should be selected because of its ability to communicate as much information as possible to expected readers of the particular paper. The author must shrewdly assess the vocabulary of the audience for this most widely distributed part of the paper. It might seem that the many prospective readers who are neither peers nor near peers ought to be given extra assistance in making their decision about whether to read further.

After all, the title will appear in many separately published indexes and thus will be exposed to many such readers. But this would require that identification of the contribution be accomplished with as little specialized language as possible. It is more reasonable that the title favor the more likely readers of the paper—the author's peers. This choice allows the author to use words and phrases that are charged with meaning for them ("key words"). Of course, needlessly specialized language can needlessly limit the audience. It is important to distinguish between terminology generally understood within an area of specialization and that understood only within a corporation, at a given university, or among those who have worked on a particular project.

Because journal paper titles are made available separately from the rest of the paper by (sometimes computerized) abstracting services, the use in the title of terms that are effectively key words also facilitates retrieval. Of course, greater accessibility has the potential of winning further recognition for the author.

### Key Words versus Buzz Words

Earlier we warned authors about the use of buzz words and now we are advocating the use of key words. There is a difference. Key words provide a means for classifying information. For example, the words "relational database" denote to computer scientists one of several basic ways of organizing electronically stored data. If the title of a paper reporting a more efficient way of retrieving stored data included this phrase, prospective readers would be helped greatly in making their decision about further reading.

Buzz words, on the other hand, are intended to evoke emotions. Fads are common in research and development, and interest may be so high in a particular area that an author may be tempted to lure readers by using some of the currently magical words in the title. At present, the letters VLSI (which stand for Very Large Scale Integration of semiconductor circuits) are in vogue. First of all, if the use of buzz words (or acronyms) is not really justified, the author's attempt to deceive readers may backfire. Even if their use is justified based on the results, as buzz words become more common, their effectiveness in selecting readers is reduced. For example, anyone doing a literature search based on the letters VLSI would discover far too many papers to be helpful.

A related tactical error is the use of "motherhood" words. A common example is the word "quality." (Who admits that they are opposed to good quality?) Similarly, in some areas that are still far from rigorously understood, it is not unusual to see the words "systematic" and "formal" used unjustifiably in attempts to garner readers.

### Other Inexactitudes

As suggested earlier, authors sometimes indicate only the area of their contributions, without identifying the contributions themselves. For example, some authors begin titles with the preposition "on," followed by words identifying a subject area; this suggests a technical essay, not a journal paper. If the author really does have an original result to report, he or she may be implying less than the paper has to offer. Vague phrases such as "design considerations about," "discussions of," and "some thoughts on" also fail to crisply identify original contributions. The word "proposal" may suggest far less than the careful analyses that we have sometimes seen following the use of this word in a title; the word proposal is associated, in the minds of some readers, with sales pitches given in efforts to win contracts. Forms of the word "design" might be more effective.

## THE ABSTRACT

The main purpose of the abstract of a primary journal paper is to further focus the reader's attention on the contribution, and thereby to help the reader to determine interest in further reading. It is even more important that the abstract be a good filter than the title. Many readers who decide to read beyond a separately published abstract will have to get access to the full paper, and more time and effort is wasted if they have made a bad decision.

Journal paper abstracts now serve an important secondary purpose. Because of the immense amount of technical information being generated, some investigators limit much of their reading to abstracts, reading more of only those few papers that are especially relevant for them. Thus, the separately published abstract becomes the basic medium through which they learn of many original contributions in their discipline.

Fortuitously, the same kinds of information are needed in the abstract to achieve both of these objectives.

### Achieving the Purposes

The word abstract denotes the separation of an idea from its surroundings, which might be its implementation in computer hardware or software, for example, or the data taken by a sociologist that gave rise to the idea. The basic idea with which a primary journal paper is concerned is, of course, an original contribution. Thus, a journal paper abstract should provide, above anything else, information about the contribution reported in the paper. The abstract usually also provides a little information about the implications of the contribution and possibly some hints about the methodology used in acquiring the new information or achieving the new result.

If some published abstracts are viewed in this light, their limited effectiveness in achieving these two objectives becomes apparent. Instead of optimizing the use of limited space, the author provides background information likely to be known by most expected readers, presents historical information, or tries to sell the results with implausible speculation about their importance. Sometimes summaries of the contents and organization of the paper are provided in its abstract, information that has value only to those who read significant portions of the paper itself. Although a case might be made for using the verbal outline type of abstract for some articles, the majority of readers of journal paper abstracts will not read much of the paper in any case. Moreover, if they understand what the contribution is and possibly the general strategy used in arriving at it, they can even guess what the structure of a relatively standardized journal paper is apt to be like.

The kinds of marginally useful information mentioned above are similar to those provided in some introductions, and indeed some authors assume that with such an abstract a conventional introduction is no longer needed. But this renders ineffective the journalistic technique we discussed at the beginning of this chapter.

Not only should most of the space in the abstract be devoted to the contribution, ideally the abstract should begin by discussing it. The first sentence can often be an expansion of the title, with succeeding sentences providing more elaboration and establishing limits. If, instead, the author builds to a climax in the abstract, busy readers, anxious to find out as quickly as possible whether they might profit from further reading, are thwarted. Many will have been required to read the entire abstract, only to learn from the last sentence that they have no further interest in the paper.

### Establishing the Limits of the Contribution

The author has a better opportunity in the abstract than in the title to communicate the magnitude of the contribution, because of the greater availability of space. As with titles, quantification is desirable where possible, but less precise comparisons are better than none at all.

Although references should not be cited, because the reference list will not usually be available to readers of separately published abstracts, alluding to the work of others is sometimes helpful in establishing the bounds of the new contribution. Such comparisons can sometimes be made by mentioning the names of other investigators or by otherwise characterizing their results.

### Indicating Significance

In discussing introductions, we distinguished between significance as measured by peers and even by near peers and that measured by wider audiences. In the widely circulated abstract, authors might be tempted to include information that appealed to larger audiences. Although some indication of significance as measured by peers and near peers might be included (straightforward practical potential, for example), catering to wider audiences here is not desirable. It not only sacrifices space that could be better used to communicate essential information about the contribution, it could alienate some readers. Some possible reasons were given in Chapter 2 for providing this kind of information in the introduction (if it is included anywhere in the paper), the most important being that space is available there to include appropriate qualification and substantiation.

### Suggesting Approaches

Many of the author's peers may be interested in the methodology used, especially if it was unconventional. Thus, a little information of this kind may also be appropriate in the abstract. As was the case with the title, adjectives such as analytical, statistical, and the like can suggest the strategy used. In some fields, standard procedures can be identified. However, methodology should only be suggested. If the author uses too many words on this subject, space is sacrificed that could be better used for describing the contribution itself.

### Writing a Terse Abstract

There are several reasons for restricting the length of an abstract. First of all, the busy reader wants to be provided quickly with exactly that information needed to identify the contribution and to determine whether to get access to the complete paper. If the author is not able to communicate efficiently the information needed for this purpose, the prospective reader has little reason to think that a better job will be done in the paper itself.

The effort involved in distilling the essence of a contribution to arrive at a terse abstract can contribute to a more effective one. There will be greater likelihood that referees and other readers will be able to determine exactly what the author has learned if it is not buried in a sea of words that the author has included to convey less important information. Material in the abstract that is not highly pertinent to the contribution can dilute its impact.

Finally, the journalistic technique mentioned earlier requires that the information about the contribution be provided with successively greater elaboration in the title, the abstract, and the introduction. As the length of the abstract approaches that of the introduction, the effectiveness of this technique is reduced. The introduction simply becomes a repetition of the abstract.

## CLOSINGS

Readers of the closing section have usually read the title and the abstract, possibly the introduction, and maybe even the body. But the last impression of the paper given to these readers, and possibly the most lasting one, will have been created by the closing.

The introduction (jointly with the title and the abstract) focused the reader's attention on the subject of the paper. The closing reverses the process, but with an important difference. The reader's thoughts are directed outward from the body by the closing, but not to the world of knowledge in general. Instead, the reader should be motivated to think about extending the author's results or of exploring alternative approaches in the same area.

There is an old adage about writing technical articles that a few of our readers may not have heard: Tell readers what you are going to tell them (the introduction); then tell it to them (the body); and finally, tell them what you have told them (the summary). This overly simple view does have some merit. One of the objectives of the closing section is to remind readers of what they have been told. Closing sections should also indicate the implications of the new results (primarily for the author's peers) and should suggest further research.

Here we consider the provision of these three kinds of information. Then we make some general comments about the writing of closings.

### Summarizing Earlier Parts

The summary portion of the closing reminds readers of how the scientific material provided in the body supported the contribution claimed in earlier parts of the paper.

Good summaries, like good introductions, are hard to write. Factors that can contribute to the difficulty include the kind of paper involved (experimental or theoretical), how well it was written up to this point, and how comfortable the author is in dealing with abstractions.

In an experimental paper, the bridge between the details in the body and the contribution claimed earlier in the paper may have been partly established before the reader has gotten to the closing. Typically, the author has interpreted the data for the reader and, in some papers, may have drawn conclusions from them. Thus, the reader's thoughts have already been brought part of the way up from the most detailed portions of the body. The author may even have discussed the broader implications of the findings. In such papers, the summary portion of the closing can often be, as the word suggests, simply a terse summing up of what has been said before. Graceful transitions may then be possible to suggestions for further work. When experimental data have been provided for their intrinsic value, a section on future research may not even be needed. However, a summary paragraph or two is still desirable to round off the presentation.

In many theoretical papers, however, the reader of the summary may have just worked through pages of mathematical or logical developments. Here the summary may have to be more interpretive. Phrases such as "it was shown that" can often begin sentences that describe how the major logical arguments presented in the body demonstrate the contribution announced in the introduction. The job is a little easier if the author has already summed up from time to time what was being proved in the body. The summary portion of the closing then becomes a summary of the little summaries that preceded it in the body.

Many authors have difficulty dealing with abstractions and tend instead to become mired in details. For example, an inexperienced author might not realize that a mathematical proof that was longer than the entire introduction might not even be mentioned in the summary. The proof might only have justified the author's use of a theorem in the body. Thus, the amount of space given to a topic earlier in the paper is not necessarily related to that given to it in the summary. It is the direct relevance of material used in demonstrating the claims made earlier that justifies its mention in the summary. In other words, the skeleton of the logic in the body, not the flesh, might be briefly summarized.

It should be noted also that a sequence of unconnected restatements of scientifically established facts is not a summary. It is the relationships among the facts and between them and the claimed contribution that must be established.

**Discussing Significance**

A kind of information that might have been hinted at in the title and the abstract and discussed in the introduction is usually treated more fully in the closing—the significance of the new results to the author's specialty. A little consideration may also be given in this discussion to the interests of near peers; for example, these readers may someday implement the newly reported ideas that have only been demonstrated in a simplified prototype by the author. However, significance as measured by readers other than peers and near peers should appear only in a separate passage in the introduction (if it is included anywhere in the paper).

The reason for deferring the discussion of significance to the closing is that the reader's greater knowledge now permits the author to point to implications of his results that the reader was not equipped to appreciate earlier. Moreover, discussions of significance in the closing often provide a smooth transition to suggestions for further research, especially since honest interpretations of new results take cognizance of their limitations.

Although restraint is still required in discussing significance, if evidence of the author's scientific integrity has been evident in the paper up to this point, he or she can afford to be a little more creative now. Of course, the author's views should be expressed as informed opinion once the realm of scientifically established facts has been left. And undisciplined "blue skying" will certainly alienate some readers.

As was the case with earlier parts of the paper, discussions of significance in closings can sound patronizing if the significance is obvious to the author's peers. The author should never appear to talk down to readers.

**Suggesting Further Research**

For the technical community as a whole, the most basic reason for journal paper publication is to reveal opportunities for further research. The investigator who has just extended knowledge in a particular area is in an excellent position to see opportunities for additional fruitful exploration. Yet, in practice, this kind of information is often omitted from journal submissions.

In Chapter 1, we mentioned that editors and referees regard "seminal" papers as being the most desirable. It is extremely difficult to guess which papers, five or ten years after their publication, will be regarded as seminal. However, by calling attention to all good opportunities for further exploration, the author can enhance whatever potential the paper has for becoming a classic.

The purpose of this part of the paper is accomplished by the author's specifically reminding readers of the boundaries of the new findings and explicitly suggesting interesting but as yet unexplored facets of the work. In identifying avenues for additional research, authors should not limit the scope of their suggestions to direct extensions of their own investigation. Indeed, the author's experience may indicate that approaches quite different from those taken might be much more productive. It is the author's professional obligation to give peers the benefit of his or her experience, even if it implies that his or her own efforts have apparently come to a dead end.

Since a basic measure of quality in a primary journal paper is the opportunities it opens, the selfless author who provides fertile discussions of such possibilities may be rewarded with a more favorable reception of the paper. In our experience, the most creative authors also seem to do the best job of suggesting further research. Perhaps they are more confident about originating even more new ideas to keep themselves busy and are thus less reluctant to share their suggestions for additional work with their professional colleagues.

**Writing the Closing**

Because successful closings are difficult to write, we add a few general comments here about their preparation. First, we consider the author's assumptions about which earlier parts of the paper may have been read. Next, we discuss the problem of avoiding boredom in reviewing familiar material. Finally, we consider appropriate verb tenses and subtitles for closing passages.

*Reading Patterns and Scientific Evidence*

Many readers of closing sections have not read the body and some may not have even read the introduction. Occasionally, authors are aware of these reading patterns and allow them to influence the way the closing is written.

But the author by now has demonstrated in the body the claims made earlier in the paper; he or she should now feel free to discuss the findings as scientifically established knowledge. To cater at this point to those readers who chose to skip earlier parts of the paper would seriously restrict the author's ability to write an effective closing. In fact, it would be difficult to determine which earlier parts of the paper might have been read. Thus, the author of a journal paper should assume that readers have read all parts of the paper up to the one currently being written.

## Avoiding Boredom

Closing sections in published journal papers are often boring, partly because of the repetition of ideas expressed earlier. Yet, the closing is essential to sum up what has been learned or done, to interpret its significance for the reader, and to suggest opportunities for further research.

The closing actually has the potential for being quite refreshing, and indeed, some closings are. Stimulating discussions of the implications of new discoveries and the opportunities they open for further exploration can be combined with terse expression and variations in phrasing to create lasting favorable impressions on the reader.

The material in the closing is often easily understood, as was the case with the introduction. Thus, the writing style suggested for introductions is appropriate here also, that is, the use of complex sentence structure to provide more information per page. But even more care should be taken here to provide information at a fast pace, because of the reader's previous exposure to much of it.

## Verb Tenses

The present tense is usually used throughout journal papers except, for example, in describing experiments that were conducted before the paper was written. The use of the present tense often even extends to the preview of the rest of the paper provided at the end of the introduction. However, the past tense is usually used in writing those parts of the closing that remind readers of what was accomplished earlier in the paper. Newly established scientific facts are an exception; the present tense is used for expressing them, since they are assumed to hold universally (that is, "it *was* shown in this paper that that condition *is* indeed always the case.").

## Subtitles

In practice, authors often use subtitles such as "summary," "concluding remarks," or "conclusions" for the closing section. We see no objection to the first two or similar subheads. However, the material provided in the closing may be much less formal than the inductive step of inferring general conclusions from experimental data. To avoid confusion, the label "conclusions" should be avoided if conclusions in the formal sense were presented in the body.

Whether separate subtitles are used for the three kinds of information that may be included in the closing is optional and usually depends on the lengths of the subsections.

## SUMMARY

In this chapter we discussed first the overlapping roles of the title, the abstract, and the introduction. We likened this redundancy to a newspaper technique in which successive presentations of a story provide readers with increasing amounts of detail. We claimed that this approach, in addition to its didactic merits, contributes to efficiency by screening out those readers not likely to profit from reading more of the paper. We also felt that this approach helps to provide readers with useful information even if they read little more of the paper.

We reminded our readers that the title and the abstract are often published separately from the rest of the paper, emphasizing the importance of these elements in selecting the audience for the complete paper. In both cases, this screening process was said to be accomplished primarily by providing information about the contribution and its bounds. Both titles and abstracts might also suggest the implications of the new results for the author's peers and near peers and the methodology used to achieve them.

Authors were advised to accomplish the purpose of the title with complete candor, promising neither no more nor no less than the paper has to offer. The attention of readers was said to be focused by classifying the area of the contribution as specifically as possible in the title without needlessly filtering out likely readers. Authors were reminded, however, that indicating the area of the contribution is not identical with identifying the contribution itself, which is the more important aim of the title. Hints at significance, we said, had to be plausible to the author's peers. Adjectives such as experimental, statistical, and the like, might be useful in suggesting methodology. The language used in the title ought to be appropriate for the audience for the particular paper.

The abstract, in addition to continuing the attention-focusing and audience filtering functions started by the title, was said also to be a basic source of information about new contributions for busy readers who are not quite interested enough to get access to the complete paper. Both purposes of the abstract were said to be achieved by providing the same kinds of information.

Authors were advised to use most of the precious space of the widely distributed abstract to describe the contribution and its limits, although significance and methodology might also be suggested. And it was recommended that authors avoid creating suspense about the contribution by the way they organize the abstract. Several reasons were given for restricting the length of the abstract.

The purpose of the closing section was said to be to direct the attention of readers outward from the body to thoughts of future research. This process was said to begin with a summary that reviews the scientific underpinnings provided in the body and their relationship to the contribution claimed earlier in the paper. The implications of the new results for the author's peers, and possibly also near peers, would then be discussed, which could provide a graceful transition to discussions of future work, which would follow.

Authors of closings were advised to be concerned about reader boredom. Stimulating discussions of further work, combined with terse expression and variations in wording from that used earlier, could make the closing one of the most interesting parts of the paper.

# 6

# *Taking and Giving Credit*

In this chapter, we consider those few elements of the journal paper that were briefly introduced in Chapter 1 but have not yet been discussed in detail. Much of our attention here is centered around taking and giving credit, and in some cases important questions of scientific rigor and of professional ethics may be involved.

We begin by discussing those parts of the paper that may in some way be related to the author's getting credit for his or her accomplishments: the author's name, the date that the manuscript was received by the journal, and the author's biography. The primary means for associating the new findings reported in journal papers with those responsible for them is through the names that appear as authors. Publication of the date that the manuscript was received by the journal provides further assurance that the author will be given credit for the discoveries, since it gives some indication of the time of their origin. The biographies usually published with journal papers provide readers with information about the authors' professional qualifications and past achievements.

We then consider those parts of the journal paper that permit the author to give credit for the ideas and work of others. References are treated first, and we include explanatory notes in this discussion because they sometimes appear within reference lists. Acknowledgments occupy our attention for the final part of the chapter.

## AUTHORS' NAMES

A few conventions have evolved in relation to the names that appear as authors of journal papers. The most important is that the named author contributed some or all of the important, original results reported in the paper. The writers of primary journal papers are not entitled to document under their names new findings that did not originate with them. To do so is un-ethical, because knowledgeable journal readers will atrribute the new ideas to the people named as authors.

Much of our attention in this section is given to this convention, includ-ing the complications arising from undeserved authorship, from ghostwrit-ing, and from reporting results of projects involving large numbers of peo-ple. Then we discuss the ordering of names in papers having more than one author and the establishment of professional identities. Finally, a potential writing problem in papers having more than one author is considered.

## Deserved and Undeserved Authorship

If only one name appears as the author of a journal paper, most likely the identified person originated the ideas and also did the writing. If more than one name appears, all those identified as authors supposedly contrib-uted, in a fundamental way, to the new findings. However, there is no nec-essary relationship among the names that appear, the order in which they appear, and the person who did the writing. The paper may actually have been written entirely by the most able writer among the investigators, or it may even have been written (although rarely) by an unidentified ghostwrit-er. In either of these cases, the real authors (those who originated the new information) may have drafted parts of the paper or at least have read and commented on its various versions.

Occasionally, some of those named as authors of journal papers have contributed little or nothing to the work. One of them may indeed have been a ghostwriter. Or an undeserving coauthor may hold a higher level po-sition in the real investigator's organization, and the supervisor may have made it clear to the subordinate that he or she expects to bask in whatever reflected glory goes with publication of the paper. Although in some cases the author may have had no choice in the matter, not all authors resist this practice as strenuously as they might. Indeed, there are cases in which the author chooses to include a superior's name on the paper, even though the superior had no part in doing the work or in providing technical guidance. The author may have been attempting to win the favor of the boss, or the boss may have a well-established professional reputation that the author hopes to exploit.

Of course, supervisors' names often appear legitimately on journal pa-pers. They may have had an important hand in initiating and directing the research. However, it should be noted that such technical leadership is dif-ferent from management or administrative support, which may, for exam-ple, have been instrumental in getting funding for the project. The latter kind of sponsorship is usually indicated in an acknowledgment section, which we discuss later.

## Ghostwriting

As indicated, we are aware of cases in which ghostwriters have been used to prepare journal papers. When this happens, the ghostwriter ought not to be rewarded by being named as one of the authors. The use of ghostwriters strikes us as irresponsible, and in any case ghostwriting does not work well in practice. The lack of intimate, deep knowledge of the work always seems to be evident. Perhaps those engaged in research and development who are willing to delegate the writing of their paper to someone else are, by the same token, unwilling to review the final product with sufficient care to ensure its authenticity.

## Reporting Results from Large Projects

Development projects are often carried out by large groups, and probably many of our readers have seen long lists of authors' names on papers stemming from such efforts. However, in a primary journal paper, only those who have contributed basic, innovative ideas are entitled to appear as authors of papers reporting the results. Work routinely expected of, say, engineers, mathematicians, or programmers does not justify listing their names as authors. Readers cannot easily determine from a long list of authors who really deserves credit or who should be consulted about the work. The goodwill felt by the real innovators toward their fellow team members should be expressed in an acknowledgment section.

## The Ordering of Authors' Names

A common problem when there is more than one author is the order in which the names should appear. The first position is generally regarded as the most prestigious. Correspondence about the work and requests for reprints of the paper are usually directed to the first named author, unless otherwise indicated. If references are made to the paper by other investigators, often only the first named author is identified, followed by "et al." Even in conversation, the author's peers may refer to the Johnson paper, with no mention of Johnson's coauthors.

When there is more than one author, the most common practices are to list the names alphabetically, to list the authors in the order of the importance of their contributions, to list first the highest ranking author in an organization, or to put the name of the actual writer of the paper first. Of course, the authors themselves must decide this question in what they believe to be a fair way, but making this decision is a potential source of friction among authors. Those involved in such controversies should remember that failure to make concessions on the current paper could lead to loss of valuable collaboration in the future.

Authors named Zworkin are at a disadvantage when names appear alphabetically. When two equally productive researchers frequently publish their results jointly, they sometimes rotate the positions of their names. We recall a case in which two authors requested that the following note be included to explain their ordering decision. "Consistent use of alphabetical ordering of authors' names tends to slight people whose names begin with letters towards the end of the alphabet. Thus, the order of names on this paper is not meant to pass judgment on the relative contributions of the authors, but rather to illustrate the fact that names appearing in alphabetical order is not a 'natural law'."[33]

## Professional Identities

An important question for authors, beyond the position of their names in a list, is the form in which their names appear. Some publications require that the name of an author appear in a certain form, for example, that only the last name be spelled out, with initials used for given names. An author whose last name is a rather common one is at a disadvantage where this practice is followed. His or her good results might be confused with those of a less competent peer having the same or a similar name. When publications do not impose such restrictions, an author who has not published before has a good opportunity to establish the name by which he or she will be known throughout his or her professional career. That name ought to be unique, if possible. Obviously authors reduce the likelihood that their names will be associated with their work if their names appear in a different form in every paper they publish.

## A Problem in Communication

In papers having multiple authors, a different kind of problem can arise that may as well be mentioned here. We recommend that one member of the team be chosen as the lead writer. This person not only assembles the pieces provided by the coauthors, but actually rewrites the entire paper. To do otherwise can lead to a subtle communication problem.

In reading journal papers having more than one author, most of us have experienced the jarring effect of passing from the material written by one author to that written by another. There is more than an esthetic problem here. Natural language is inherently imprecise,[27] but readers seem to adjust to the way that individual authors express themselves. Even if the writing does not denote precisely what the author intended, the reader often realizes what was actually meant. The next author, with another unique personal style, expresses the same ideas slightly differently, and the reader must readjust to that style. But if one person does all the writing (or rewrites everything drafted by coauthors), this barrier to communication is lowered. Because of the difficult material often provided in journal papers, this and any other opportunity to make matters easier for the reader should be exploited.

## MANUSCRIPT RECEIPT DATE

Independent research often results in two or more investigators making similar discoveries at about the same time. This is not surprising when one considers the effort often concentrated in narrow areas of investigation. Because the results of research are sometimes not patentable, the date that a manuscript was received by a journal may be the sole means for estimating the time of a discovery. Most primary journals publish that date, and possibly also the date when a major revision was received (typically, after refereeing). These dates are imperfect indicators of primacy, of course, because a manuscript may have been submitted to but rejected by other publications or the author may have had the results long before the manuscript was submitted. But these dates are the only tangible evidence that the rest of the world has about the times of origin of many new discoveries. (It is obvious that authors who indefinitely postpone documenting their results risk being preempted.)

Receipt dates can also be used by authors to determine the average time to publication in a particular journal. The shorter that time, the lower the probability of being "scooped" by publication of similar results from another investigator.

Incidentally, wise editors sidestep controversies about the time of origin of ideas, since they are not equipped to gather and evaluate evidence and they have no legal standing to judge such matters. If they learn, soon enough, that another author has beaten their author into print with a very similar result, they simply reject the paper. There is little point, therefore, in an author's complaining to an editor if he or she thinks that a professional colleague has behaved unethically.

This may be an appropriate time to add that discretion by a researcher in revealing new results informally and privately is occasionally good preventative medicine. Most researchers behave ethically, but not quite all of them.

## PROFESSIONAL BIOGRAPHIES

Ideally, readers of primary journals, in assessing the results of research and development, are influenced solely by the scientific evidence presented in the paper. Actually, the credence of the author is established partly by the information provided about his or her academic and professional background in a biographical sketch (*curriculum vitae*), as well as by his or her reputation. None of this material is scientific evidence, but it would be unrealistic to think that it has no effect on the reaction of readers to an author's claims of new findings. In fact, readers of journal papers must accept a good deal on faith. For example, if there is no reason for suspicion, they usually accept the author's experimental data as being correct. They simply do not have the time and resources to examine in detail every professional colleague's corroborative evidence or to duplicate the work. Biographical information is another indication of the reliability of the new information, although some of the author's peers will view the biography itself with as much professional skepticism as other parts of the paper.

The author's biography is written as though someone other than the author had prepared it. However, everyone associated with journals knows that the author really did the writing, a fact that should be remembered in its preparation. If an author gives the appearance of exaggeration in the biography, some readers may conclude that claims of new results may also be extravagant.

The purpose of the professional biography is achieved by providing information that is relevant for readers who are assessing the qualifications of the author to do the work needed to achieve the original results reported in the paper. Thus, professional biographies usually indicate the kind of work the author is now doing and a brief history of professional experience. Teaching assignments, sabbaticals at research establishments, and widely recognized professional achievements are usually included. Relevant educational background is, of course, provided, including the dates that degrees were received and the institutions that awarded them. Significant academic honors may also be mentioned. Well known awards are often listed, and memberships and honorary positions in professional societies are also indicated.

However, if there is any question about the prestige associated with an award, it is better not to mention it. For example, most members of the author's profession may have no idea of the criteria applied in bestowing an award within a corporation or of the meaning of an honorary title at a particular university.

The professional biography should also omit those aspects of the author's history that have no bearing on the work. For example, marital status, past athletic achievements, or military awards are not usually relevant. Memberships or offices held in organizations unrelated to the author's professional life, such as political posts, are also excluded.

Unduly long biographies, especially ones padded with trivial accomplishments, can be a source of embarrassment. We recall an instance in which an author unblushingly described himself as the father of the subspecialty in which he worked. Even if this had been the case (he probably was the oldest), the author might have chosen more modest phrasing, such as "has long been identified with . . . ."

Although it is in the author's interest to include all significant achievements, slight understatement is to be desired in author-written biographies.

## REFERENCES AND FOOTNOTES

References in primary journal papers confront authors with problems that are not encountered in most other kinds of factual writing. It was necessary when we discussed introductions in Chapter 2 to mention the three main purposes that references might serve in journal papers: to compare a new contribution with those previously reported in the formal literature; to allow authors to include information substantiated by other investigators; and, least important, to direct readers to additional information. Not only do references serve additional purposes in journal papers, there are sometimes restrictions on the sources of information that ought to be referred to.

We first remind readers of the role of the primary journal paper in an effort to show its effect on the use of references. We then expand our earlier discussion of the three main functions of references and follow that by considering some situations in which the author may refer to less formal sources of information, including conversations, personal correspondence, patents, and papers that have not yet been published. Suggestions follow on ways that references can be cited in text and described in reference lists to make them more useful to readers. Observations are also included about hidden messages that editors and referees may see in the reference list in a journal paper. Finally, some opinions about footnotes are offered.

### Building the Knowledge Base

Each paper published in a primary journal represents a formal contribution of knowledge to the author's discipline. The new findings are based on results that have been substantiated and documented by other investigators; future contributions, in turn, will probably be based on the author's discoveries.

The requirement of scientific rigor in journal papers sometimes limits the extent to which an author's discoveries can be based on information that has not been subjected to the testing that journal publication implies. This sometimes restricts the documents that can be referred to. For example, it may not always be appropriate to repeat in a journal assertions that were made elsewhere without scientific proof. Thus, the author of a journal paper must be aware of whether he or she is referring to a formal document, that is, a journal paper, or to a less well-tested source of information. For example, in referring to a book, it may be important for the journal author to know whether an opinion of the author of the book is being repeated or a scientifically established fact is being restated.

### Referring to Related Work

As indicated in our discussion of introductions, in order for independent referees and other readers to evaluate contributions documented in journal papers, they must be able to see exactly how far present knowledge is extended by the new results. Thus, referring to related work can be a descriptive technique to help readers to understand the character and extent of an original contribution.

We suggested in Chapter 2 that authors not be content simply to cite a group of references at the end of the first sentence to achieve this purpose. Actually, new results can best be integrated into the knowledge base associated with a particular discipline if the author goes even beyond inserting a reference identifier here and there in the description of the contribution. Relationships with prior results can be better established by actually adding appropriate words and phrases, such as "Brown's survey, on the other hand, indicated that . . . ," "this is an increase of 13 percent over that obtained using the method of Smith . . . ," and "instead of the 16-bit addresses used in the earlier processor. . . ."

In fitting new findings into the context of present knowledge, formal documents are usually referred to. Unsubstantiated information obtained from less formal sources does not provide a sound base for comparison. Occasionally, however, discoveries described in journal papers may have been motivated by less formal sources of information. For example, the author may have carried out research suggested in some other kind of a technical article, such as a survey paper or a technical essay, and thus refer to that document in the introduction of the paper. In this case, however, the author is not using the cited work as a basis for comparison but to give credit for the suggestion.

## Using the Ideas of Other Investigators

Information that appears in journal papers ranges in a continuum from unsubstantiated opinion to experimentally verified scientific facts, although it is convenient here for us to place it into several distinct categories. In all cases, the author is required to help the reader to determine just how much confidence to put in the information that was included in or referred to in the paper.

Again, authors who include unsubstantiated opinions of their own or of others must inform readers of that fact. New information that did originate with the author must, of course, be substantiated in the paper. Information that has long been accepted in the discipline may also be included, and in this case the author is not even obliged to cite a reference for it. But if information is included that has been recently substantiated in other formal documents, the author is obliged to cite the source of the information, both to justify its use in the paper and to give credit to its originators. Because ideas that are neither accepted generally in the discipline nor attributed to another researcher are assumed to have originated with the author, failure to attribute them properly is a breach of professional ethics.

If the author uses words rather than simply inserting reference identifiers, the reader can see exactly how much of what is being said is due to the other investigator. For example, the author might say "Seddon found that introduction of the catalyst reduced time for the process by 17 percent" or "Lacy demonstrated in his Theorem 4 that . . . ."

Formal documents are usually referred to so as to justify the inclusion of scientifically verified information. However, the author may refer in an incidental way to less well substantiated information if it is not part of the foundation for his or her own results. But the author is obliged to help readers to determine how much stock to put in the information. For example, a phrase might be included, such as "Foley suggests, as a possible explanation for this phenomenon, that . . . ." The caveats "suggests" and "possible" convey the idea that Foley is only expressing an opinion.

It should be noted, incidentally, that in the physical sciences, engineering, and mathematics, the ideas of other researchers are typically not quoted but paraphrased. We do not know the origin of this practice. However, by paraphrasing the ideas in his or her own style, the author not only communicates the information but also demonstrates that it has been correctly interpreted.

### Suggesting Sources of Additional Information

The author's peers are the primary audience for the journal paper, and they are assumed to be familiar with the current literature in their area of specialization. Thus, there would seem to be little need to direct such readers to sources of additional information. Moreover, if the author does refer to additional sources of information, the presence of these references and their citations can create difficulties for the reader who is attempting to see how the new result fits into the fabric of present knowledge.

For these two reasons—the limited need by typical journal readers for background information and the fact that referring to it can get in the way of satisfying another reader need—the omission of all such references from journal papers would seem to be justified. Indeed, references to further information often do not appear in journal papers.

However, even the most conscientious journal readers have difficulty staying current in a world of rapid technological progress. Also, there is often need for communication across discipline boundaries. Indeed, the paper itself may represent an interdisciplinary contribution in which the audience cannot be assumed to be completely knowledgeable. Students and recent students may also need extra assistance.

For all of these readers, then, it may sometimes be reasonable to provide references to background literature when it is most relevant for them, that is, when it is needed to understand a paper reporting a new result in which they are interested. The author of the journal paper would seem to be the best qualified person to identify the most valuable and reliable sources of such information.

The interests of those readers of journal papers who are not completely conversant with the literature in the subject area can be satisfied without sacrificing other reader needs if the author indicates the nature of the reference in the text where it is cited. For example, the author can insert phrases such as "additional information about these polymers is provided in . . ." or "Klokholm surveyed the literature in this area in . . . ." If the author has followed the same practice in citing references for other purposes, the references to further information should create no confusion for readers.

Sources of background information can also be provided in a list of general references or in a bibliography, separated from the references that were cited for other purposes. The author may indicate their presence at an appropriate place early in the paper.

Sources of additional information are likely to be survey or review papers, rather than formal documents. Because readers of such documents are presumably less well equipped to detect technical flaws in them, it is especially important that the author refer only to reliable sources.

## Referring to Less Formal Documents

In a number of situations, the author of a journal paper may refer to less formal sources of information. These include references to earlier announcements of the results documented in the current paper, to patents, to information acquired by the author through private sources, and even to papers that have not yet been published.

### Referring to Earlier Versions of the Paper

It is not unusual for an original contribution to be announced in a published abstract, a conference paper, or a "communication" or "note," such as those published in *Applied Physics Letters*.[2] Such documents make the new results available to the author's peers more quickly than formal journal publication. However, these announcements are typically shorter than journal papers, do not include as much scientific substantiation, and may be subjected to less rigorous or no refereeing.

When such publication has preceded formal submission to a journal, the author usually cites the earlier document in the paper. A footnote on the first page is often used for this purpose. Phrases may be used such as "a preliminary version of the results documented here appeared in . . . ." Alternatively, the earlier article may be cited as the first reference, near the beginning of the introduction.

Referring to the earlier announcement of a new result serves at least two purposes. It suggests an earlier date for the author's discovery, which may influence whether he or she is given credit for originating the new information if another researcher publishes a similar result at about the same time. It also reduces the likelihood that journal readers will think that the author is attempting to publish the same results more than once or to republish someone else's results. Readers may vaguely recall having read something about the contribution before. The reference tells them explicitly that it was the author's own informal announcement of the contribution.

## Referring to Patents

Some information included in journal papers may have been made known previously in a patent. A reference to a patent should identify the person to whom the patent was issued and should provide its title, its number, and its date of issue.

Patents, like early announcements, associate ideas with their originators by date and thus help to ensure that the author is given appropriate credit.

It may be interesting to note that patents are not regarded as formal documents in the sense that journal papers are. Many patents may be issued for different implementations of the same basic idea, but, in principle, only one journal paper should document an original idea. Publication of a journal paper is justified to report a new implementation only if it is both innovative and nontrivial.

## Referring to Other Informal Sources

The author of a journal paper may have gotten information in other informal ways: from company documents not available to readers, from correspondence, through conversation, and from papers that have not yet been published.

Credit is usually given for an idea acquired directly from its originator by following the statement in the text with a citation (and possibly other information) and then including in the reference list the name of its originator followed by the words "private communication." Unless the credited colleague is very well known in the field, his or her affiliation should be provided to ensure that credit for the idea is attributed rightfully and so that readers can contact the originator of the idea if they should choose to do so. Authors sometimes show the relevant material to its originator if it did not originally exist in written form so that he or she can confirm its accuracy.

An obvious problem with such references is that no corroboration is available to the journal reader. The requirement for scientific rigor would not be satisfied if the author's results depended too directly on such unsubstantiated information. Thus, such references are usually included only to treat a professional colleague fairly and not as a base for building new results.

No purpose is served by referring to documents that are not available to readers. If an idea from such a source is used, the author of the journal paper can attribute it to its originator as a private communication.

*Referring to Documents Not Yet Published*

An author may be aware that especially relevant work is slated for publication in the future. In this case, there may be insufficient information for a complete reference, but the author may use the phrase "to appear," with as much information as is available. To avoid an awkward situation, the author should try to be sure that no last minute problem is likely to prevent publication of the paper referred to. It is for this reason that we feel uncomfortable about another phrase sometimes seen in reference lists: "submitted to." If the submitted paper is never published, the author of the newer paper is placed in an awkward predicament. Moreover, some doubt is raised about the new results if they are built on the material referred to.

## Citing References

Throughout the discussion of references, we suggested that authors include more than a simple reference identifier. We have another reason for making that recommendation. Many readers of journal papers turn to the reference list as soon as they encounter a citation. This is often necessary because of the multiple purposes of references in journal papers and because each new paper must be integrated into the body of literature associated with the discipline. However, the inconvenience for readers of looking back at the reference list is apparent.

This inconvenience can be eliminated if information that is likely to satisfy the expected interests of readers is provided where the reference is cited. Most readers will probably recognize the related work from the name of the person responsible for it or through some other suitable characterization of it, rather than just a reference identifier. Phrases may be included such as "Ames concluded that . . . ," "when Haiber simulated this phenomenon, he found that . . . ," and "our process improves semiconductor yield by 7 percent over that described by Evans."

*The Mechanics of Citing References*

A few basic styles are used to cite references in journal papers. For example, a number, corresponding to the location of a reference in a list near the end of the paper, may be included in square brackets (to distinguish reference citations from equation numbers, which are often included in parentheses). Or the reference number may appear as a superscript. (To avoid confusion, an attempt should be made to separate numerical identifiers from mathematical expressions.) References are sometimes cited by using the last name of the author, or the first few characters of the last name, followed by the last two digits of the year of publication. If the author of the cited paper has published more than once in a given year, other codes are devised to uniquely identify the reference.

Techniques that do not require the renumbering of all subsequent references if a reference is added are convenient for the author during manuscript preparation. However, the style used by an author should correspond with that used in the journal for which the paper is intended. If the author chooses to use a scheme that is more convenient during the writing process, he or she can convert to the preferred style before actual submission.

## Providing Useful Information about Referenced Documents

There is considerable variation in the format preferred in reference lists in particular publications. We are not concerned here with the relative merits of these methods. However, the fundamental purpose of the information provided is to facilitate acquisition of the material referred to, and all information needed for that purpose should be provided, even if there is some redundancy. For example, the volume number and the year of publication of most periodicals is redundant, but including both may be helpful to readers. The volume number might readily be seen on the spine of a journal stored on a shelf, but the year might be more useful in identifying a bound volume. The issue number within the year and the date of issue may be redundant. However, quarterly issues may typically be referred to by number, whereas monthly issues may be identified by the name of the month of issue. Because it is sometimes difficult to anticipate what information is most useful to readers, a little duplication does not seem to be such a bad thing.

In some disciplines, titles are typically omitted from references. Despite the prevalence of this practice, it obviously creates an avoidable problem for the reader. The name of the author must be associated with the particular work referred to, and the reader may have to distinguish by date or by publication among several papers by the same author.

The value to readers of providing page numbers or other internal signposts to identify passages within longer documents is obvious.

## Unexpected Information Acquired from References

Because editors and referees are obliged to read many papers, they usually develop some shortcuts to assist themselves in making appraisals. References are one of the first things examined, and they can be surprisingly informative. Obviously, if the reader is at all familiar with the subject area, the references provide some help in identifying the contribution. No references, too few references, or references limited to papers that have all appeared in the same journal may suggest to referees and editors that the author is not broadly acquainted with related work in the field. Old references may indicate that the author's knowledge of related work is not current. If most of the references are to secondary sources and to textbooks, the author may not even be aware of his or her obligation to fit new results into the fabric of current knowledge. If there are many references, the author may not have done a good job of finding the exact niche into which the contribution fits. If most of the references are to earlier papers of the author, he or she may be promoting a career, rather than fulfilling obligations to readers.

Editors also look at references to help identify potential referees for the paper, since the references may form a ready list of active workers in the author's area of specialization.

## Footnotes

Explanatory notes are sometimes provided at the bottom of the page (the foot) in which they are cited. A symbol, such as an asterisk, a dagger, or a lower case letter, is typically inserted in the text to direct the attention of the reader to the corresponding symbol at the bottom of the page and thus to the material in the note.

Footnotes create page layout problems (which may not concern the author). The page on which the footnote is to appear cannot be determined until the pages are laid out. If the footnote symbol appears near enough to the end of the page, there will not be enough room left for the footnote itself.

But there is a better reason for avoiding footnotes. When readers encounter a footnote symbol, they are being directed to something supposedly important enough to justify interrupting their reading. After readers have finished with the footnote, they must find their place in the text and resume reading. If the material in the footnote really is important enough to justify the interruption, an effort should be made to include it in the text parenthetically. However, there are cases (material containing mathematics, for example) in which a footnote may be the only reasonable way of providing relevant information.

Explanatory notes and other less relevant observations are sometimes included among the references, instead of in footnotes. Diverting the attention of readers to them causes an even greater interruption.

## ACKNOWLEDGMENTS

Many research and development projects could not have been carried out without the dedicated assistance of a large cast of supporting players. The conducting of tests, the writing of computer programs, the compilation of data, the interviewing of subjects may all have been essential to the success of the endeavor. Even though the supporting players did not contribute original ideas that would justify listing them as coauthors, it is common practice to give them credit in an acknowledgment section.

Authors may not realize the importance that others attach to seeing their names in an acknowledgment section. These people may never publish a paper themselves, and this is one of the few instances in which they will see their names in print. Even if the author's motives are completely selfish, remembering this assistance may ensure cooperation in the future. The author can reduce the likelihood of overlooking a participant if the work is reviewed chronologically before the paper is submitted.

Tactful authors avoid making unintentional comparisons in their acknowledgments. Moreover, they try to err in the direction of generosity. But there are limits. We recall a single-spaced acknowledgment section that extended over two full pages. After thanking numerous colleagues, his wife for typing many drafts of the paper, and his children for not disturbing him while he was working on it, the author elaborately thanked God for the abilities that enabled him to do the research and to write up the results. This is the closest that any author in our experience has come to claiming a divinely inspired paper.

## Remembering Referees

Referees are the unsung heroes and heroines of the journal publication process. Occasionally, their assistance is so exceptional that the author feels obliged to express gratitude with the other acknowledgments. For example, a referee might have furnished a more direct mathematical proof or pointed out a serious error. Authors can give credit to the anonymous referee in their acknowledgments by indicating, instead of the referee's name, some clue about the nature of the assistance. At least the anonymous referee knows that the help is appreciated.

Some grateful authors go beyond an acknowledgment in the paper. We have sometimes been asked to forward messages of gratitude to referees for unusual assistance. We have even seen the names of referees added as coauthors because of the value of their help. In such cases, the editor acts as the go-between, requesting that the referee agree to divulge his or her identity.

## Acknowledging Funding

Much research is supported by funds provided by governmental bodies or philanthropic institutions. The recipient of such support may also express gratitude in the acknowledgment section. Some researchers have a contractual obligation to do so. Instead, a footnote on the first page is sometimes required.

## SUMMARY

In this chapter, authors' names were discussed first, and we said that the owner of a name appearing as an author of a journal paper was assumed by its readers to be responsible for some or all of the original results reported. In papers having more than one author, the ordering of the authors' names was said to be unrelated to who wrote the paper, which on rare occasions might actually have been done by an unnamed ghostwriter. However, readers were reminded that the well established convention linking authorship with responsibility for original ideas was sometimes violated by listing undeserving people as authors.

Significant concerns of journal authors were said to include the order in which their names are listed on papers having more than one author and the form in which the names appear. Beginning authors were advised to seek a unique name form to establish their professional identities.

The date that a manuscript is received by a journal was said to be a measure, although an imperfect one, of the time of the author's discovery. A revision date (typically, after refereeing) might suggest when significant new material was added.

Professional biographies were said to be the primary source of information about the author's professional credentials. Only information relevant in establishing the author's qualifications should be included, and modesty was suggested for the author-written biography.

We reminded readers that references might be included to indicate sources of further information, to help describe the contribution, and to justify the building of new results on the work of other investigators. We also noted that a reference might be included to an earlier, less formal announcement of the contribution and to such other sources of information as private communications. Authors were advised not to be content simply with a citation but to include more specific information in the text about the cited work. Some remarks were also made about the insights that the reference list might provide to referees and editors.

It was suggested that authors consider including footnote material parenthetically in the text wherever possible, as an alternative to interrupting readers' concentration.

Acknowledgments were said to provide a mechanism for giving credit to the many people who may have assisted the author in getting the results. It was suggested that authors avoid unintentional comparisons and to err in the direction of generosity. Exceptional help from referees might also be noted. The author was reminded of possible contractual obligations to acknowledge sponsorship of research.

# *Appendix A*

## CHECKLIST FOR INTRODUCTIONS

After having read the introduction, will the author's peers
  Understand exactly the nature and extent of the contribution?
  See its relationship to current related knowledge?
  Have sufficient background information to appreciate its significance?
  Have some understanding of its implications for the discipline?
  Have a little knowledge of the methodology used?
  Know something about the structure and contents of the rest of the paper?

Regardless of the kind of opening used,
  Has a terse summary of the contribution been provided?
  Was it provided as soon as readers could assimilate it?
  Was it assumed that readers knew nothing about it from having read the title and the abstract?
  Has the description been confused by the inclusion of any other kinds of information?
  Was the opening that was chosen appropriate for the contribution?

If the statement-of-the-contribution beginning was selected,
  Has sufficient context been established for the author's peers to understand the nature of the contribution?
  Have enough details been provided for them to understand its exact scope?
  Has explicit consideration of significance been excluded from the description?

If the historical opening was chosen,
  Is the history really appropriate for the audience?
  Is it more extensive than really needed for readers to understand the nature of the contribution?

If the statement-of-the-problem opening was used,
  Is the problem either a classical one or one little understood by the author's peers?
  If the problem is a classical one, has it been identified as soon as possible?
  Have readers been told as quickly as possible that the problem was solved?
  If the problem is not generally understood, is its description nonetheless no more elaborate than it need be?
  Has the breadth of applicability of the solution been communicated?

If the statement-of-objectives beginning was used,
  Have the achievements been summarized in a terse statement announcing the contribution?

Is each objective and achievement really unique?
Do readers always know and agree with the rationale for the objectives?
Does the list of achievements sound promotional?
Do explanations of failures sound like alibis?

In describing the contribution,
Has it been integrated into the body of current knowledge by references?
Are comparisons fair to other researchers?

If background information is included,
Is it really needed by the intended audience to understand the nature of the contribution?
Has credit been given for information taken from other sources?
Has background material been labeled so that it can be skipped by those who do not need it?

If the significance of the contribution is explicitly discussed,
Has the discussion been clearly separated from other information?
Is it directed to a single audience?
Is there any possibility that it will alienate the author's peers?
Are opinions distinguishable from facts?

If methodology is mentioned,
Is the discussion sufficiently brief to be included in the introduction?

If the rest of the paper is previewed,
Is the preview the final item in the introduction?
Is the rationale for the structure of the paper sufficiently obvious or should it be suggested?

In writing the introduction,
Has the author kept the pace at which information is provided appropriate, based on its complexity?
Have general statements been suitably qualified?
Has too much detail been provided too soon?
Will anything sound trite or patronizing to the author's peers?
Is the entire introduction sufficiently free from salesmanship so as not to offend the author's peers?

# *Appendix B*

## CHECKLIST FOR THEORETICAL PASSAGES

Has the theory been organized so that it leads as directly as possible to the author's conclusions?

Has the reader been told beforehand about the organization and its rationale?

If top-down organization was used, has subject matter been divided into too many (more than seven) or too few pieces, and have the divisions been made at logical places?

Have readers been reminded at the beginning of lower level passages of their relationships to information provided at the next higher one?

Could the exposition have been enhanced by a running example or by figures?

Has anything not essential to understanding been retained simply because the author knows it?

Was the mention of alternative reasoning strategies really necessary and, if so, was it disposed of quickly?

Have readers always been made aware of what is being proved?

Would readers understand and agree with the assumptions on which the logic is based?

Have all facts required to follow the author's reasoning been provided?

Have the facts been provided in context and at the point where they were needed whenever possible?

Have readers been required needlessly to memorize symbol definitions or abbreviations?

If a glossary was provided, have symbols also been defined near where they were used?

Have symbols been chosen that are consistent with those conventionally used in the discipline?

Have nonstandard symbols been chosen that suggest their meaning?

Has the same symbol been given more than one meaning?

Is specialized language widely understood among expected readers?

Has efficient specialized language been needlessly avoided?

Has less formal logic been provided as tersely as possible?

Have examples been used to lend concreteness to abstract ideas?

Have readers been thoughtlessly required to solve puzzles?

Have mathematical developments been carried to, but not beyond, a level needed by the audience?

Have readers been warned that unconventional approaches were taken?

Has useful but currently unessential information needlessly intruded into logical developments?

Has enough information been provided to demonstrate practicality if that is a claim?

# *Appendix C*

## CHECKLIST FOR EXPERIMENTAL MATERIAL

Do readers know what purpose is served by each experiment?

Are readers likely to be convinced that the experiments described can produce the data claimed for them?

If negative results were mentioned, were they disposed of quickly?

Will the statistical characteristics claimed for data be accepted by competent statisticians?

Are descriptions of equipment and procedures sufficiently detailed to allow competent readers to duplicate the experiments without being encumbered by needless details?

Have all factors that might have influenced results been explicitly accounted for?

Have sufficient data been presented to justify any significance that has been attached to them?

Have some raw data been provided?

Have the data been provided in ways that best reveal their significance?

Are figures overly complex?

Are captions as helpful as possible to readers?

Have observations been supported by actual data?

Have inferences been confirmed by sufficient experimentation?

Will the reader always know when the author is expressing opinions?

Has the author communicated the broader significance of the results to peers?

# Notes

1. Bernard Houghton, *Scientific Periodicals—Their Historical Development, Characteristics and Control* (London: Linnet Book & Clive Bingley, 1975).
2. *Applied Physics Letters* (New York: American Institute of Physics).
3. *Scholarly Communications—The Report of the National Enquiry* (Baltimore: The Johns Hopkins University Press, 1979).
4. Sydney Passman, *Scientific and Technical Communication* (Elmsford, N.Y.: Pergamon Press, 1969).
5. *Encyclopaedia Britannica,* Vol. 8 (Chicago: Encyclopaedia Britannica, 1967), p. 650.
6. Ludovico Geymonat, *Galileo Galilei* (New York: McGraw-Hill, 1965).
7. William Broad and Nicholas Wade, *Betrayers of the Truth: Fraud and Deceit in the Halls of Science* (New York: Simon and Schuster, 1983).
8. H. J. Tichy, *Effective Writing for Engineers, Managers, Scientists* (New York: John Wiley and Sons, 1967).
9. William Strunk, Jr., and E. B. White, *The Elements of Style* (New York: Macmillan, 1972).
10. *A Manual for Authors of Mathematical Papers* (Providence, R.I.: American Mathematical Society, 1978).
11. *Handbook for Authors of Papers in American Chemical Society Publications* (Washington, D. C.: American Chemical Society Publications, 1978).
12. *Style Manual for Guidance in Preparation of Papers for Journals Published by the American Institute of Physics* (New York: American Institute of Physics, 1963).
13. *Publication Manual of the American Psychological Association* (Washington, D. C.: American Psychological Association, 1983).
14. Michael J. Katz, *Elements of the Scientific Paper* (New Haven, Conn.: Yale University Press, 1985).
15. Robert A. Day, *How to Write and Publish a Scientific Paper* (Philadelphia: ISI Press, 1979).
16. Herbert B. Michaelson, *How to Write and Publish Engineering Papers and Reports* (Philadelphia: ISI Press, 1982).
17. *Style Manual for Biological Journals* (Washington, D. C.: American Institute of Biological Sciences, 1964).
18. John Stuart Mill, *Philosophy of Scientific Method* (New York: Hafner Press, 1950).
19. Peter Caws, *The Philosophy of Science, A Systematic Account* (Princeton, N.J.: Van Nostrand, 1965).
20. Roderick Chisholm, *Theory of Knowledge* (Englewood Cliffs, N.J.: Prentice-Hall, 1977).
21. Sidney Morgenbesser, ed., *Philosophy of Science Today* (New York: Basic Books, 1967).
22. George A. Miller, "The Magic Number Seven, Plus or Minus Two," *Psychological Review* 63 (1956): 81-97.

23. John F. Sowa, *Conceptual Structures: Information Processing in Mind and Machine* (Reading, Mass.: Addison-Wesley, 1984).
24. J. W. Backus, "The Syntax and Semantics of the Proposed International Algebraic Language of the Zurich ACM-GAMM Conference," in the *Proceedings of the International Conference on Information Processing, UNESCO, Paris 1959* (London: Butterworths, 1960), pp. 125-32.
25. W. J. Plath, "REQUEST: A Natural Language Question-Answering System," *IBM Journal of Research and Development* 20, no. 4 (July 1976): 326-35.
26. Martin Schatzoff, "Design of Experiments in Computer Performance Evaluation," *IBM Journal of Research and Development* 25, no. 6 (November 1981): 848-59.
27. Wilfrid J. Dixon and Frank J. Massey, Jr., *Introduction to Statistical Analysis* (New York: McGraw-Hill, 1969).
28. Norman L. Johnson and Fred C. Leone, *Statistics and Experimental Design in Engineering and Physical Sciences* (New York: John Wiley and Sons, 1964).
29. Taro Yamane, *Statistics, An Introductory Analysis* (New York: Harper and Row, 1964).
30. D. C. Baird, *Experimentation: An Introduction to Measurement Theory and Experiment Design* (Englewood Cliffs, N.J.: Prentice-Hall, 1962).
31. Christian K. Arnold, "The Construction of Statistical Tables," *IRE Transactions on Engineering Writing and Speech* EWS-5, no. 1 (August 1962).
32. Edward R. Tufte, *The Visual Display of Quantitative Information* (Cheshire, Conn.: Graphics Press, 1983).
33. M. A. Wesley and G. Markowsky, "Fleshing Out Projections," *IBM Journal of Research and Development* 25, no. 6 (November 1981): 934.

# *Index*

## A

Abstract models, 54
abstract models as data sources, 69-70
abstracts, 19; achieving the purposes of, 91-92; establishing limits in, 92; indicating methodology in, 93; indicating significance in, 92; need for terse writing in, 93; primary purpose of, 91; purposes of, 83-84; secondary purpose of, 91; suspense in, 92
acknowledgments, 20,113; for funding, 114; for help from referees, 114
algorithms, 59
announcing contributions, 24
application of theory, 61
approaches used to get new results, 41
assumptions, explicit statement of, 51-52; justification of, 51; underlying logic, 19-20; underlying mathematics, 51
audience needs for background information, 36
author's biographies, 21, 104
authors' names, 18, 100; ordering of, 102
authorship, deserved and undeserved, 101
autobiographical descriptions of reasoning, 50

## B

Background information, 34
background sections in introductions, 29
biographies, authors', 21,104
black box articles, 45, 52
body of the journal paper, 19
bottom-up organization, 49

brevity, limits on, 14, 51; need for in abstracts, 93
brute force solutions, 7
buzz words in titles, 90

## C

Cache memory, 87
career promotion in journal papers, 11
characteristics of journal papers, 8
checklists, for experimental material, 121; for introductions, 117; for theoretical material, 119
citing references, 31-32, 111
claiming new results, 24
classical problems, 28
closings, 20, 93; avoiding boredom in, 97; subtitles in, 97; writing style for, 96
communications, 4, 109
complex sentences in introductions, 42
computer generated data, 75
computer simulation as a data source, 69-70
conceptual background information, 35
concreteness in abstract material, 58-59
conference proceedings, 4
contentions to be proved, 19, 50
contributions, definition of, 24; identification of, 84
controlled experiments, 9
correctness of new results, 3
criteria for publication, 6
criticism, author reaction to, 62

## D

Date of manuscript receipt, 21, 104
dealing with abstractions, 95
defining terms, 54

deriving meaning from experimental data, 77
describing work, 24
design of experiments, 70
difficulties of new authors, 8
difficulties in writing introductions, 23
digressive material, handling of, 60
dilution by irrelevant information, 13
distinguishing original ideas, 25


**E**

Efficiency in journal papers, 8, 12
elegant results, 7
elements of the journal paper, 17
epistemology, 8
ethical lapses, 11; consequences of, 12
evenness of presentation, 59
exaggerated claims in experimental papers, 80
excessive rigidity in writing, 15
expectations of the introduction, 25
experimental apparatus, 20
experimental conditions affecting data, 76
experimental configurations, 71
experimental data, broader implications of, 20, 79; computer generation of, 75; deriving meaning from, 77; ease of comparison, 75; excessive amounts of, 74; inferences from, 77; interpretation of, 75; observations derived from, 77; opinions based on, 78; presentation of, 72; in raw form, 73; restrictions on publication of, 74; in summarized form, 73; too little of, 74; uncertainties in, 68
experimental design, justification of, 68
experimental evidence, 19
experimental information, categories of, 66
experimental papers, function of, 65
experimental procedures, 20, 72

experimentation, 46; to confirm hypotheses, 67; negative results of, 67; to obtain useful data, 67
experiments, purposes of, 20, 66
expressing opinions in journal papers, 40


**F**

Facts, needed for understanding, 19, 53; treatment of, 54
factual background information, 35
failing to identify contributions, 24
falsifying experimental results, 11
faulty related work, 33
figure captions, 77
figures, needless complexity in, 76
filtering process of opening parts, 19
focusing readers' attention, 18
footnotes, 113; to tables, 76; in theoretical passages, 50
formal publication, 3
further research, 96


**G**

Generality of contributions, 28
ghostwriting of journal papers, 102
glossaries, 56
graphs, designing and labeling of, 75


**H**

Headings in experimental papers, 66
hierarchical organization, 48; problems with, 48
historical openings, 26


**I**

Identifying contributions, 84; topics to be covered, 15; to reinforce organi-

[Identifying contributions]
    zation, 48-49; to show experimental
    set-ups, 71
implications of experimental results, 79
imprecision in titles, 90
inferring conclusion from experimental
    data, 77
information retrieval systems, 32
integrating new results into present
    knowledge, 31
interdisciplinary contributions, 29
introductions in journal papers, 19
introductory material throughout pa-
    pers, 14
irrelevant information, in journal pa-
    pers, 13; in theoretical material, 49
isolating background information, 36

**J**

Jargon, 57
journal paper beginnings, 25; intro-
    ductions, 24
journalism technique used in journal
    papers, 84
judging contributions, 6
justification for experiments, 20

**K**

Key words in titles, 90
knowing the literature, 32

**L**

Language suitable for titles, 89
level of detail in theoretical material,
    59
limitations of new results,
    40
literature searches, 32
lucid writing, need for, 14

**M**

Manuscript receipt date, 104
mathematics, stating purpose of, 50;
    writing of, 58
measures of significance, 37
methodology, suggesting in abstracts,
    93; suggesting in title, 89; used to
    get new results, 41
methodology papers, 53
missing references, 33
mixing motives in writing, 25
mock-ups as data sources, 69
models, relationship to reality, 53
"motherhood" words in titles, 90
multiple contributions, 24

**N**

Names of authors, 18, 100
near peers, 38
negative experimental results, 67
notation, mathematical, 54, 55
notes, 4, 109
numerical methods as data sources, 69

**O**

Observations from experimental data,
    77
opening parts of journal papers, 83
opening words for introductions, 30
openings, historical, 26; statement of
    the contribution, 25; statement of
    objectives, 29; statement of the
    problem, 27
opinions based on experimental data,
    78
ordering of authors' names, 102
organization, bottom-up, 49; hierarchi-
    cal, 48; limitations of, 49; prefer-
    ence for simpler, 47; rationale for,
    48; reinforcing of, 48-49; of title,

[organization]
abstract, and introduction, 84; top-down, 49
organizing, of documents, 15; experimental papers, 66; theoretical material, 47
orientation of readers, 51, 66
originality of results, 3, 5
outlines of documents, 15
outlining paper in abstract, 19
overcoming mind set, 60

**P**

Page charges, 13
paper tigers, 62
parenthetical observations in theoretical passages, 50
parts of the journal paper, 17
peer review, 3
perceived importance of contribution, 28
permission to reprint, 35
pitfalls in introductions, 30
planned redundancy, 14
plausibility of claimed significance, 40
postponing discussions of alternatives, 50
predictions based on experimental data, 77
preliminary findings, 4
presenting experimental data, 20, 72
prestigious journals, 7
previewing the paper, 19, 41
previously unidentified problems, 29
primary journal, definition of, 1
private communication, 110
probabilistic models, 69-70
professional ethics, 8, 11
professional identities, 103
promotional arguments, 10
prototypes as data sources, 69
purpose in writing, 15
purpose of the introduction, 23
purposes of experiments, 20
purposes of references, 31
puzzles in theoretical material, 59

**Q**

Qualitative experimental results, 68
quality of writing, 7
quantifying new results, 26, 31
quantitative experimental results, 69

**R**

Reader reaction, sampling of, 61
received dates of manuscripts, 21
red herrings in theoretical passages, 50
redundancy, planned, 14
refereeing, value of, 3
refereeing process, 3
referees, acknowledging help from, 114
references, as basis for describing new results, 107; citing of, 111; to documents not yet published, 111; documents that can be referred to, 107; to earlier versions of paper, 109; to further information, 31, 108; to informal sources, 110; to patents, 110; purposes of, 20, 31, 106; to related results, 31; unexpected information from, 112; useful information about, 112; to work and ideas of others, 31, 107
rejection, of experimental papers, 80; of theoretical papers, 62
related literature, 4
relating contributions to present knowledge, 31
relevant factors in experimental set-ups, 71
repetition, justifiable, 14, 52, 83; needless, 76
reportable results, 5
requesting reprints, 35
"respectable" journals, 12
restrictions on publishing data, 74
review papers, 4
running examples, 48

**S**

Sales literature, 12
sampling reader reaction, 61

scientific method, 8
scientific rigor, 8
seminal papers, 7, 96
significance, discussing in closings, 95; indicating in abstracts, 92; indicating in titles, 88; of new results, 2-3, 36-37; of practical results, 37; to wider audiences, 38; where to treat, 40; writing style when discussing, 95
sources of uncertainty in data, 69
sponsors of research, 39
standardizing journal papers, 15, 16
statement-of-contribution opening, 25
statement-of-objectives opening, 29
statement-of-problem opening, 27
statistics, ignorance of, 70
straightforward organization, 47
subject matter, division of, 48
subtle implications of new results, 37
summaries, 94
summarized experimental data, 73
superfluous information in journal papers, 13
survey papers, 4
suspense in journal papers, 29, 30
syllogisms, 51
symbols, conventional usage of, 56; definition of, 55; selection of, 56; substituting for words, 56

**T**

Tandem models as data sources, 70
technical essays, 5
terminology, impressive sounding, 57; knowledge of, 57; misuse of, 57
terseness, limits on, 14, 51
testing process in journal publication, 3
theoretical arguments, 19-20; constructs, 46; developments, 19
theoretical material, 46; categories of, 47; irrelevant information in, 49; purpose of, 47; puzzles in, 59; specialized facts in, 54
theory, application of, 61
titles, 18, 84; bad impressions from, 85; candor in, 85; establishing limit

[titles] in, 87; focusing on area of contribution, 87; humor in, 85; identifying contributions in, 87; imprecision in, 90; indicating significance in, 88; language for, 85, 89; "motherhood" words in, 90; plausibility of, 88; purpose of, 83; responsibility for misinterpretation of, 85; suggesting methodology in, 89; underselling results in, 86; unfulfilled promises of, 86
top-down organization, 49
transferable technology, 5, 54
treating significance, 39
tutorials, 5

**U**

Unflattering comparisons with other work, 33
unjustified theoretical claims, 80
unscientific evidence, 9

**V**

Verb tenses in journal papers, 97

**W**

Weaknesses, in historical openings, 27; in problem statement openings, 28; in statement-of-contribution openings, 26; in statement-of-objectives openings, 29
window dressing in theoretical passages, 50
withholding currently unneeded information, 49
withholding facts until needed, 55
work in progress, 4
working documents, 7
work load of the author, 16
writing, jointly authored papers, 103; of journal papers, 15; the introduction, 42; less formal logic, 58; mathematical material, 58; process of, 15; style for closings, 96

# *About the Author*

Since graduating from Hofstra University in 1949, Sylvester P. Carter has spent his entire professional life in writing and editing. He has been a technical writer at Westinghouse Electric Company and at Norden Laboratories. His career includes six years on the staff of the McGraw-Hill magazine, *Electronics*, and four on the *IBM Systems Journal*. Mr. Carter has been an associate editor of the *IBM Journal of Research and Development* for sixteen years.

Carter, Sylvester P.
  Writing for your peers.